Haiku Master Buson

TRANSLATIONS FROM THE WRITINGS OF YOSA BUSON
—POET AND ARTIST—
WITH RELATED MATERIALS

YUKI SAWA
&
EDITH MARCOMBE SHIFFERT

Companions for the Journey Series, Volume 13

WHITE PINE PRESS / BUFFALO, NEW YORK

This book, in slighty different form, was originally published in 1978 by Heian
International Publishing Company.

Publication of this book was made possible, in part, by public funds from the
New York State Council on the Arts, a State Agency,
and a grant from the National Endowment for the Arts,
which believes that a great nation deserves great art.

Cover art: Detail from a painting by Yusa Buson.

First Edition

Companions for the Journey, Volume 13

10-digit ISBN: 1-893996-81-6
13-digit ISBN: 978-1-893996-81-6

Library of Congress Control Number: 2007921245

Published by
White Pine Press
P.O. Box 236
Buffalo, New York 14201
www.whitepine.org

"What you want to acquire, you should dare to acquire by any means. What you want to see, even though it is with difficulty, you should see. You should not let it pass, thinking there will be another chance to see it or to acquire it. It is quite unusual to have a second chance to materialize your desire."

—Yosa Buson
"New Flower Picking"

CONTENTS

Essays on Buson by Kito

PREFACE

Although Yosa Buson is considered to be one of the three most celebrated haiku poets, along with Basho and Issa, this is the first book in English to be concerned entirely with his writings. Buson was an artist who painted untiringly throughout his lifetime, but he was also a constant and sincere poet of haiku. Some two thousand eight hundred fifty-two of his haiku exist today. From these, a sampling of about three hundred seventy-five have been translated for this book.

For those unfamiliar with the conventions of haiku and its 5-7-5 syllable form, the books by Harold G. Henderson are a good introduction. Those by Makoto Ueda are excellent for a deeper understanding of the significance of haiku and

Japanese aesthetics.

Buson's three long poems have also been translated for this book. They are considered to be a combination of both haiku and Chinese styles of poetry. They are the only non-haiku poems written by him except for the *renga* that he often did with friends. For each such poem, he wrote some of the 5-7-5 or 7-7 syllable sections required to make a long cooperative piece.

Sometimes Buson wrote a preface for a friend's book or a few commentaries on the haiku of his contemporaries. He was not primarily a prose writer, and perhaps, the most interesting of these writings are his letters. Three hundred fifty-seven of them are known. The principal letter collection belongs to the Tenri Library, Tenri City, Nara, and there exist a number of unauthenticated Buson letters. Material by Buson is now highly valued by collectors.

The original of "A Record of the Rebuilding of Basho's Grass Hut" is owned by Konpukuji, Kyoto, the temple where what is called Basho's Hut is located and where Buson is buried. This temple also has several items done by, or once belonging to, Buson.

The brief essay "Visiting Uji" reveals the old poet in his final year enjoying his last outing. Kito's "Record of Buson's Last Days" is translated here because it gives a first-hand picture of the old poet and the affectionate respect of his friends and disciples. It helps us to realize anew that Buson's haiku was written two hundred years ago in the then isolated country of Japan, and that he was aware of an older Japan and China.

The translators have included a brief biography of Buson, an introductory essay and brief essays at the beginning of each of "The Seasons of Haiku" by Edith Shiffert, and an essay by Yuki Sawa titled "Buson and his Writings." Supplemental reading material is listed at the end of the book.

In this book, the Japanese names have been given in the Japanese manner, family name first. Although he is primarily known as Yosa Buson, at various times he used different names, most notably Saicho, Yahantei, and Shikoan. His paintings were signed with a number of names, including Shunsei, Nodojin, and Shain.

Japanese dates are approximate. In Buson's time a lunar calendar was used, and the year began about a month and a half later than it does now.

Although in the original Japanese some of the haiku have brief explanatory prefaces, only those that might be of interest to non-Japanese readers have been included.

The haiku presented here are in the same order as in *Buson Zenshu*, Volume I, edited by Dr. Ehara Taizo, published in 1948. Although the haiku texts are mainly taken from the above mentioned book, they are also, at times, based on other versions, such as those in *Busonshu*, by Prof. Teruoka Yasutaka (1959) and *Busonshu-zen*, by Profs. Otani Tokuzo, Okada Rihei, and Shimasue Kiyoshi (1972).

Some Japanese words that are now used internationally, such as *geisha*, *go* and *koto*, have not been translated here.

However, it should be mentioned that an *ayu* is a trout-like fish and *uguisu* and *hototogisu* are names of birds. In the section of translated haiku, notations appearing as titles above some of the poems are Buson's. Comments by the translators are in brackets.

Introduction

Edith Shiffert

A collection from the haiku of Buson can be a partial portrayal of the daily life of Japan about two hundred years ago, in the Edo, or Tokugawa, period. In many ways, it is still the Japan of today, or life as known anywhere, and it will be familiar and recognizable. Naturally, the more a reader is familiar with each haiku's scene, the more pleasure it will give him; and the more haiku he has read by one particular poet, the more he will recognize the personality of the writer. The feeling of knowing what is depicted—recognizing it, sharing it—is one of the satisfactions found in reading this seventeen syllable and seemingly quite limited literary form.

On examining the poems as they are presented here, in the order of the seasons, there seems to have been a consciousness of the lengthening or shortening of daylight hours, as well as a consciousness, sometimes stylized, of the general passage of time and one's life. Then as now, it was a special pleasure to quietly spend a day or two at a country inn or temple with a good friend. Taking short walks, sake drinking, talking, poetry writing, perhaps sketching, sometimes being playful with the waitresses and hostesses, or just looking at nature in places that other poets and artists had enjoyed was sufficient. A number of Buson's haiku give glimpses of such occasions in all seasons.

Although pheasants are rather rare today in Japan, in some areas they may rise up when startled by a passerby; the fox is supposed to have supernatural powers and to be a specialist in transformation, as well as a messenger of the gods. Japanese artists have often painted foxes as ethereal beings of great beauty and mystery, and from ancient time they were associated with Shinto religion and folk beliefs as both reality and symbol. The nobleman who is really a fox could be imagined as perhaps someone so elaborately dressed as to seem illusionary.

The burning of incense was manifold: in temples, before graves, at the Buddhist altars within homes, or for the aesthetic pleasure of appreciating fragrance. Punk-like insect repellents were also burned.

As the most common means of going places was by walking, Edo people became completely familiar with their neighborhood and its shortcuts through the fields. In most rural areas, houses were clustered together, usually along a road, with their rice fields and vegetable gardens along the road or nearby. Long journeys were made on horseback. Small boats crossed rivers too deep for wading; during heavy rains, streams were frequently flooded and dangerous. Palanquins were sometimes used, too, but when traveling, Buson writes most often about walking or riding horses or taking ferryboats. Boats were also for pleasure: to the old Chinese poets, whom Buson admired and wished to resemble in the simple graces of their lives, drifting in one on a warm day with a friend while writing poems was an aesthetic pastime.

Buson often shows a sense of humor, and we should remember that there was a tradition of vulgar haiku and senryu in which any obscenity was allowable. Some of these haiku are very human, and their humor can still be appreciated. Traces of such attitudes can sometimes be found in

Buson's haiku and in brush sketches that depict the common people in the midst of their activities. It is obvious that he felt warmly toward these people; perhaps, in a way, he considered himself one of them. Perhaps, his showing of things as they are can be a Zen-style revealing of reality or a comical ridiculing of pomposities; humor as a leveler that keeps man alert and humble, reminding him of his physical and social limitations.

In the prose selections translated from *New Flower Picking*, the piece about staying at a temple called Kenshoji is an example of the humor popular at that time in tales and verse. Several different meanings can be given to the works used in the haiku in this piece; its Rabelaisian character is, perhaps, partly a result of its being a satire on too much sentimental writing of poetry on every occasion. The brief tales in *New Flower Picking* were from Buson's personal memories, and he put them into his notebook after discontinuing it as a haiku-diary. They show something of the ordinary life of the Edo period. Even a poet as serious as Buson did not hesitate to use vulgar humor and was fascinated by popular folk beliefs, such as supernatural foxes and badgers. Perhaps a ghost story that also included a temple priest and some embarrassment handled humorously was considered especially entertaining, the kind of true story that is still frequently told as a social pastime. If Buson disapproved of vulgar material, it was for aesthetic reasons rather than moral ones; he was not a stranger to the available pleasures of his time.

More often, we find in Buson's brief poems an aesthetic

and sensuous appreciation of his existence. That Chinese poets and artists and the seventeenth century poet Basho were his ideals gives a distinctive quality to his best pieces, which usually seek the quiet and simple as in the Taoist-Buddhist tradition. The many uses of moonlight, different for each season, express his rich awareness of the ordinary, and through a seemingly spontaneous selection of detail, we are given moments eternalized. Tenderness, too, can often be felt in his words, for the people and for life itself. Though he rarely expresses the philosophic melancholy or spiritual aspirations of Basho, he depicts the material scene with the voice of a sensitive artist. Intelligent, poor, existing as best he can in the limitations and pressures of Edo society, he is mostly uncomplaining and stubbornly productive as artist, poet, and a living human. It is easy to feel affection for the man we can imagine him to have been as glimpsed through his writing, art work, and what we can know today of the existence that was the subject of his expression. Through his haiku and paintings, through what we still see that is hardly different in either Japanese or universal life, we may imagine him as real as these things are.

Using poetry writing as his meditation medium, a poet can be aware of many things, especially of his own being as a part of all being, its unique particularities, and its inescapable oneness with the cycles of nature. The preface to the *Collected Haiku of Shundei* is a prose example of Buson's writing that tells how to make poems as the great poets did.

Each poem is unique in its choice of images and the way

they are presented. It will be seen that, at times, the same word has been given different translations. *Hito*, for example, may be expressed in English as someone, a man, a person, people, humans. The untranslatable parts—expressions such as *kana* or *ya*, called cutting words *(kireji)*—are represented here as a dash, comma, semicolon, exclamation mark, a word, or simply ignored. These translations are a loose approximation of the originals rather than something done by positive decisive rules. A translator can only grope hopefully for the meaning of each piece, trying not to be a machine of production, but seeking words and patterns that will make a poetry yet not be "poetic." Of course, it cannot be done easily, if at all. To give hundreds of poems all in the same exact brief form, often on similar themes, without sounding either repetitious or tricky is almost unavoidable. One can only try to concentrate on what it was that gave them value when first written. To attempt to be brilliant or innovative would seem out of place. Neither just concentrating on linguistics and words, nor just seeking some mystic rapport with the original writer, nor just making a great creative effort can achieve good translation. All methods must be combined, in varying degrees, with one's innate ability and luck.

The Japanese originals remain the ideal presentation, but with the *romaji* accompanying each poem, it is possible for a reader to make his own variations. We should not forget that Buson was indeed skillful in the art and craft of his language and this poetic form, but even in translation, it is possible to appreciate his creations for what they reveal of himself and his world and of his awareness as an artist. We can positively have the images Buson had, inasmuch as we can comprehend the words of a poet of any language, including our own. Also, inconsistencies in translation help avoid giving an over-formalized impression of Buson's haiku. Using different *kanji* and *hiragana* and, sometimes, *katakana* character combinations, he himself rewrote the same haiku on different occasions, such as making a copy for a friend or writing it in an album.

The poets had a relaxed approach to each other— friends sharing food and wine, often teasing and joking, though at times talking seriously, sympathizingly, or melancholically. And haiku writing can be a kind of lone meditation, a moment of realizing actual life.

For a number of these haiku, explanations have been written; some are enjoyable or revealing, though not essential for comprehension; some are pedantic and conflicting, done by competing specialists; some sermonize or simplify for children; and some intelligently add to the meager hints given in a haiku. The same has been done with Western poetry, and indeed, this essay is a further example of superfluous comment. But human beings are talkers, and haiku are short enough to leave time and space for more words. The most loved work of the master Basho himself, *The Narrow Road to the Deep North*, sets haiku in the midst of narration. Short poems surrounded by prose has always been one of the most used styles of Japanese writing. It is found in the eighth-century *Kojiki*, the first Japanese book, and remains prevalent in the literature of the Heian period and afterwards.

In every season, Buson was conscious of the farmers and the rice fields. These same rural scenes can still be seen, visible even from clusters of large, newly built apartment houses in the suburbs. Remnants of old life styles exist side by side with the new. Rice growing has always required cooperative work, and in Edo times, even a divorced wife had to contribute her labor to the community work done on her former husband's land, just as today a vacationing university student may help his family on visits home. Women workers on the land still wear special working costumes, and the birds and most insects still come, though fireflies have disappeared from many areas.

Many of the haiku can be variously interpreted. Take four consecutive ones for example. First, a flying bat causes a neighbor's wife to look in his direction. Is this merely pictorial, erotic, humorous, or the unpredictability of existence? We are given no hint. Secondly, someone leaves fish at the gate late at night. Is this a thank-you poem or a vivid little night scene? Then, the grasping of a firefly while in a dark mood might be an abstraction or actual night and a small light or unexpressable grief. Lastly, the firefly burning before a Buddha image might be a pictorialization of a rural night scene, a concept of the insect as sacrifice or offering or devotion, a sudden realization of life as a momentary burning before the Buddha, fate, or the eternal. It is up to each reader to find what he will, but perhaps with some awareness of what Buson as a sensitive eighteenth century man and a constantly developing painter intended. Perhaps one truth of haiku is that all the potential interpretations do exist in the poem inasmuch as they are in the actual things written about and that the words do not obtrude on these possible and contradictory imaginings about the poem.

In Buson's time, social positions were rigidly fixed: the government was all-pervading and religion taught acceptance of one's fate. At times nature was violent. Yet, the race survived, and flowers bloomed at expected times and places year after year. And the common man developed the rough humor that became the cheerfulness of the poor. Buson was never a wealthy man; until he was sixty he lived in what could be called poverty. However, he seems to have made his own adjustments to a way that allowed him to do his work quite freely, to feel the dignity of an imagined alliance with the artist-poets of old China as well as Japan's great philosopher-poet Basho, and to be a happy man who in the latter part of his life had the respect and affection of a group who considered him their master in poetry and painting. Usually this seems to have been enough for him, though in his letters he sometimes complains of his poverty. At least in his haiku we do not find expression of the spiritual sufferings of Basho nor of Basho's yearnings for a purification. Buson utilized his own senses in creativity, and this must have given sufficient satisfaction to prevent any real passivity even within the structural limitations of his society.

Judging from his paintings, he must have had considerable powers of sustained concentration. The constantly developing changes in his painting styles give evidence that his thought on this work was continuous. Perhaps this is one reason why his haiku could seem so relaxed and yet, at the same time, be of high artistic quality.

> By lightning
> the small house was burned down
> and now melon flowers!

We should remember that Buson was aware of Chinese philosophy and art, that he spent about five years living in temples, and that he was a lay priest of the Pure Land sect of Buddhism. In signing the long poem "Mourning for the Old Poet Hokuju," he calls himself "Priest Buson."

The easily available books on Japanese history by G.B. Sansom as well as Edwin O. Reischauer describe the political and cultural background of Buson's time. They also tell enough about Pure Land Buddhism to make his role as a lay priest more understandable. In that popular form of Buddhism, it was believed that a priest should go on with his life in the same way as other men. There is no evidence of Buson having had a temple of his own or functioning as a priest. It seems to have been a personal matter, perhaps one of convenience, a role in the government's formalization of society. Basho had also been a lay priest.

Remarks scattered throughout the writings of Buson and his friends show him to have been a sophisticated man well aware of his position as artist and poet. Often, he was more of a cynic than a romantic. His best poems may have been a form of personal solace. Since he managed to support himself and his family as a painter, he was able to avoid the common custom of the haiku master being a popular teacher and corrector of haiku. He expressed his scorn for what he considered haiku-degrading work, done to please whatever group was being addressed. Yet, his humility in saying that he could not write the excellent haiku he aspired to as a follower of Basho reveals his deep artistic urge and sincerity.

In an art exhibition in the 1970s, there were a number of fans, scrolls, and poem cards mounted for hanging on which were written famous haiku by Basho and Buson; some were done in their own brush writing and some in that of their disciples. Often, a small picture, sometimes in colors, had been added with the writing brush by one of the two renowned poets or a friend. The brush writing of Basho showed delicate and fine lines, suggesting something of fragility or spirituality; that of Buson was always heavily done in thicker black strokes, seeming masculine and sure. Buson's reverence for Basho was shown by the many copies he had made of his work. There was a scroll done by Buson, some twenty feet or more long, of Basho's most noted book, *The Narrow Road to the Deep North* [Oku-no-Hosomichi]. Buson had copied the text by hand and had alternated it with illustrations shrewdly imagined. At first, they seem mainly humorous and cartoon-like, but on careful observation, they express a tenderness and warmth for Basho's experiences. Actually, Buson depicted the people—country priests, village women, farmers, rural poets, young waitresses, porters, foot travelers, people at various kinds of work—as they actually were. Buson shows them each in a particular moment of their lives, usually in combination with several other people and Basho, who was the traveler and honored poet-guest. How active and lively human they have all remained through Buson's insight into the sources of Basho's writings.

It is interesting to note that Basho himself in a painting accompanying his famed haiku has shown not only one crow but a flock of crows perched in the tree and whirling about in the sky just above:

> On a withered branch
> a crow has settled—
> twilight in autumn.

And the autumn tree is hung with bright persimmons, a very different interpretation than the lonely melancholy one usually given to this poem. Which is the "right" way to think of it? Perhaps both or neither? A reader usually assumed the thing written about in a haiku was singular unless specified as otherwise, since the whole attitude of haiku is one of focusing on the particular in a certain moment. It is only one crow and the tree is bare; this must be assumed by the translator, although the noun does not usually indicate whether it is singular or plural. In translating Buson's several haiku about peonies for instance, a non-Japanese hesitates between whether Buson was seeing one or several. After seeing these haiku paintings where numerous crows and violets in the mountain pass are shown, it can be realized that, although in the actual poem a single flower is usually assumed, the poet could have been seeing many. For a painting to be most effective, more than one may be necessary; for a poem, just one. But this is not necessarily a positive matter.

A number of Buson's haiku resemble details of his paintings, from the huge elegant multipanel screens to the cartoon-like brush sketches of Edo-times people. His landscape paintings can be lofty and mystical in the Chinese way or very Japanese in the style he gradually developed and perfected for depicting villages and the countryside, mountains and water, birds, trees, streets, people and their homes.

Included in this book is a translation of Buson's own explanation of a place known as Basho's Hut. It still exists in northeast Kyoto at the base of one of Mt. Hiei's foothills. It is in the garden of the old temple of Konpukuji, which was originally Tendai, or esoteric Buddhist, but Zen since before the time of Basho. Here, on a winter day, it is easy to imagine Buson's world. In a hall of the small temple, a warmly robed old priest sits on a floor-cushion at a low table where stationery and booklets describing the place are sold. When several people have entered in their stocking feet and knelt to inspect the mementos displayed concerning Basho, Buson, and a romantic couple once also associated with the temple, he sets a tape going that tells the history of the place. The south wall will be left open if the sun is shining, and the priest will have a charcoal firepot beside him; there may even be one for visitors to briefly warm their fingers. Outside is a formal garden of sand and carefully shaped hedges of ever-green azaleas. A few yards up the slope can be seen the roof of Basho's hut and, beyond it, a small forested mountain. The foliage is dense, even in winter, and though roads with traffic and new houses are just outside, they are not visible.

At the top of a winding path of stone steps is the hut, rebuilt, of course, not only since Basho's time but also since Buson's. It is pleasant to sit on the edge of the narrow veranda of five planks alternated with four lengths of bamboo and try to understand something more of Buson. He knew this place two hundred years earlier, thought of it as one favored by Basho, and loved it enough to ask to be buried here. The eaves project about five feet from the four walls of the square hut, and the roof of closely layered reeds resting on a web of bamboo poles is about two feet thick and the color of sand or old reeds by a pond in winter. The earth-plastered walls rest on small rocks, but under them and the eaves is a con-crete slab that surely wasn't there in Buson's day. The walls are broken in places, and the supporting corner posts are full of small holes and indentations made by insects, sometimes forming a natural design that resembles calligraphy. At the south window, the shutter that is covered with cedar bark is propped open with a bamboo pole, and the paper-covered panels on the south and north have been slid open to show a straw-matted room about nine by twelve feet in size. In the *tokonoma* is an ordinary vase of a cut section of bamboo in which someone, perhaps the wife of the temple priest, has placed several sprigs of small white flowers.

It is easy to realize why Buson could have favored this place even in winter. The wind from the north and east is stopped by the slopes of Mt. Hiei. A warmth of sunlight floods in from south and west. Across the basin of Kyoto city, the mountains rise clearly, each forested ridge distinct, the tops whitened with snow so that they look higher than they are. Buson could write the same kinds of poems today as he did in the eighteenth century. Sitting here alone or meeting with a few friends, the same kinds of poetic gentlemen or ladies who may still be found existing in Kyoto, the same subjects and responses might come naturally to one filled with the tradition of haiku and a fondness for old Chinese poetry. The ancient capital of a thousand years ago, now a modern city of a million, spreads out just below, invisible in valley haze, the physical shape of its enclosing landscape unchanged.

Another short path leads upward to Buson's grave. All around, native shrubs grow thickly with mosses, ferns, and pampas grass. Gigantic camphor trees retain their leaves in winter. A few *sasanqua*, or camellias, will be found flowering on even the coldest days. Though the place is rarely crowded, there are always a few quiet visitors throughout the daylight hours when the temple is open. Their behavior is similar to what Westerners consider appropriate for visiting cathedrals. Some quote haiku by Basho or Buson, and it is apparent that the place is visited as a respected shrine as well as for its scenic beauty and age. The slopes above are still heavily forested, and flocks of birds fly in and out more noisily than the distant traffic. Buson's grave is in the shaded forest, and the graves of friends and other later poets are nearby, outlined and marked by rough-cut greyish stone. The western mountains and afternoon sun can be glimpsed through tall old pines. A red pine just behind his grave-marking stone bends upward for some seventy-five feet like a dragon, centuries of growth compressed in its twisted trunk. Throughout spring, both the wild and the cultivated azaleas will be blooming there profusely. In summer, the dense shade from the overhead trees and a slight mountainside breeze make it as cool a place as any. In the bright autumn days of sunlight and red leaves, it is warm enough there to comfortably sit outside for hours.

> I too when dead
> want to be near this stone marker—
> the withered pampas grass.

SPRING

In a collection, haiku are customarily arranged according to season, beginning with spring—which used to start on New Year's Day according to the old lunar calendar.

The first haiku writing of the new year was especially noted, often done in the company of a friend or other poets, and accompanied by modest eating and drinking in a quiet place, such as the home of one of them. The men would, of course, be wearing kimono, and small charcoal braziers would warm their hands and feet. If the day was sunny, the sliding panels along one wall of the room would be opened to let in the natural warmth. From such a common scene could have come the first haiku presented in this book; either Buson or another poet he knew may be glimpsed, a bit humorously, making his New Year poem.

> The year's first poem done
> with self-confidence—
> a haiku master.

Even today in Kyoto, haiku poets make an occasion of writing the new year's first poem, and they visit each other, walking through the chilly streets where there may be patches of fog. Though there are no longer boundary guards, each traffic guard at a railroad crossing, as well as innumerable watchmen, has a charcoal firepot, or perhaps an electric or oil heater, in the little shelter where he spends the working day.

Anyone who has spent a year in Japan will recognize Buson's spring rain; how it touches everything, joins together

32

pond and river, yet is light enough so that a frog may be able to keep his belly dry—his own back serving as a rain-cape or umbrella. The soft mists and fogs of spring merge with the brief cherry blossoms, a warmer sensuous time. Farmers do their work while the *uguisu*, a small greenish-brown bird, a bush warbler, sings its spring song. To those who have often heard this bird, just its name evokes a countryside scene with all its scents, sounds, colors, movements, and vegetation— thatched roofed farmhouses in a valley, a temple or shrine visible among them, a green forested mountainside in the background, weather, and the air itself that is being breathed. A consciousness of continuity to life and, at the same time, a sort of timelessness may be sensed in such poems. It is possible that Buson was aware of this and, as a craftsman, sought appropriate ways to express it. Haiku do not usually give an open statement of a poet's opinions, but by what he chooses to include in a haiku, the "egoless" poet is known.

There are swallows, too, and fish and frogs and butterflies. The Japanese language used in describing these is not sentimental but realistic, so that we know the actual quality of each creature. The butterfly on the neckplate of an ambushed warrior's armor or on a temple bell, a plum flower lying upon a horse's droppings, show a conscious artistic manipulation that Buson does not abuse. Some who try to imitate him may overemphasize this sort of juxtapositioning of the unexpected or highly contrasted, but Buson's haiku are more often of the expected, the usual, as known in a still moment fully experienced.

Spring Haiku

The year's first poem done
with smug self-confidence—
a haikai poet.

Saitan o shitarigaonaru haikaishi.

New Year's Day
and on the day after,
fog from place to place in Kyoto.

Ganjitsu futsuka kyo no sumizumi kasumikeri.

The boundary guard's
small charcoal firepot,
the lingering cold.

Sekimori no hibachi chiisaki yokan kana.

Daylight longer!
A pheasant has fluttered down
onto the bridge.

Osoki hi ya kiji no oriiru hashi no ue

Yearning for the Past
Lengthening days
accummulate—farther off
the days of long ago!

(Kaikyu)
Osoki hi no tsumorite toki mukashi kana

Slowly passing days,
their echoings are heard
here in Kyoto.

Osoki hi ya kodama kikoyuru kyo no sumi

(Visiting Wakinohama Beach with Kito)
The slanted way
the sleeping quilts have been placed
at dusk in spring.

(Kito to Wakinohama ni aso bishi toki)
Sujikai ni futon shikitari yoi no har

The white elbow
of a priest who is dozing!
Dusk in spring.

Hiji shiroki so no karine ya yoi no haru

Into a nobleman
a fox has changed himself—
early evening of spring.

Kindachi ni kitsune baketari yoi no haru

In a casual way
incense in being burned—
day's end in spring!

Naozarini ko taku haru no yube kana

At dusk in spring
the almost completely burned
incense, replenished.

Haru no yube taenan to suru ko o tsugu

The light of a candle
is transferred to another candle—
spring twilight.

Shoku no hi o shoku ni utsusu ya haru no yu

A short nap, then
awakening—the spring
day darkened.

Utatane no samureba haru no hi kuretari

The scented clothes
still not put away,
twilight in spring.

Nioiaru kinu mo tatamuzu haur no kure

Who is it for,
the small bed pillow,
twilight in spring?

Tagatame no hikuki makura zo haru no kure

The big gateway's
massive doors—
spring twilight.

Daimon no omoki tobira ya haru no kure

In the springtime dusk,
distant from the homeward road,
people wandering.

Haru no kure ieji ni toki hito bakari

Only today left
of spring. My walking
ended it.

Kyo nomi no haru o aruite shimaikeri

The foot washing
tub has a leak too—
spring is running out.

Senzoku no tarai mo morite yuku haru ya

Yesterday ended,
today again there will be an end—
spring is waning.

Kino jure kyo mata kurete yuku haru ya

The going of spring!
The heaviness of a mandolin
felt while it is held.

Yuku haru ya omotaki biwa no daki gokoro

Spring Twilight
Spring is going;
hesitating and indecisive,
the last cherry blossoms.

(Boshun)
Yuku haru ya shunjun toshite oso zakura

The going of spring!
The purple fading away
from Tsukuba mountain.

Yuku haru ya murasaki samuru Tsukuba yama

Reclining Buddha,
its carving just finished,
and the end of spring.

Nebotoke o kizami shimaeba haru kurenu

Spring is going,
we cannot know where—
the anchored boat.

Yuku haru no izuchi iniken kakaribune

Walking on, walking on,
things wondered about—spring,
where has it gone?

Aruku aruki mono omou haru no yukue kana

Color and fragrance
of a figure seen leaving—
the going of spring.

Iro mo kamo ushirosugata yo yayoijin

With a woman companion,
bowing respectfully by the Imperial Palace;
clouds over the moon.

Onna gushite dairi ogaman oborozuki

His baggy trousers
pushed off with his foot tonight—
a hazed-over moon.

Sashinuki o ashi de nugu yo ya oborozuki

Fragrance of incense
around a man while he naps—
a cloudy moon.

Kyarakusaki hito no karine ya oborozuki

Pillowed on my arm
I feel loved for my own self—
a hazed-over moon.

Tamakura ni mi on aisu nari oborozuki

Hazy moonlight!
Someone is standing
among the pear trees.

Oboroyo ya hito tatazumeru nashi no sono

On Kawachi Road!
An east wind of spring blowing
a shrine maidens' sleeves.

Kawachiji ya kochi fuki okuru miko no sode

Without underwear
a bottom blown bare of robes—
the spring wind.

Fudoshi senu shiri fukare yuku ya haru no kaze

The springtime rain!
Someone is living there now,
smoke leaks through the wall.

Harusame ya hito sumite keburi kabe o moru

Springtime rain!
Almost dark, and yet
today still lingers.

Harusame ya kurenan-toshite kyo mo ari

A springtime rain!
Little shells on a small beach,
enough to moisten them.

Harusame ya koiso no kogai nururu hodo

Poem in a Dream
Springtime rain,
and impossible for me to write—
how sad it is.

(Muchugin)
Harusame ya mono kakanumi no aware naru

Spring rainy season!
Talking together passing by,
straw cape and umbrella.

Harusame ya monogatariyuku mono to kasa

The pond and the river
have joined together as one
in the spring rain.

Ike to kawa hitotusu ni narinu haru no ame

Spring rain;
the belly of the frog
not wetted.

Harusame ya kawazu no hara wa mada nurezu

A Korean ship
passes by without stopping here,
misty weather!

Komabune no yarade sugiyuku kasumi kana

View of a Field
Grasses in a mist
and water flowing silently,
daylight fading!

(Yabo)
Kusa kasumi mizu ni koe naki higure kana

A mountain temple—
a bell struck clumsily
resounds blurred in the fog.

Yamadera ya tsukisokonai no kane kasumu

In the Suburbs
In shimmering air—
insects I cannot name,
whiteness afloat.

(Kogai)
Kagero ya namoshiranu mushi no shiroki tobu

Heat waves in the air—
and a basket full of the earth
which the man loves.

Kagero ya ajika ni tsuchi o mezuru hito

A spring stream
in country without mountains,
flowing on smoothly!

Haru no mizu yama naki kuni o nagare keri

No bridge for crossing
and the day coming to an end—
the river in spring.

Hashi nakute hi kuren to suru haru no mizu

Delicate legs
wading through stir up the mud
in the springtime stream.

Ashiyowa no watarite nigoru haru no mizu

Water of spring,
violets and white flowered reeds
moistened as it flows.

Haru no mizu sumire tsubana o nurashiyuku

In a boat at noon
an insane woman riding—
springtime waters.

Hirubune ni kyojo nose tari haru no mizu

The springtime sea
all the day long tossing
and tossing!

Haur no umi hinemosu notari-notari kana

Beds of young rice plants—
Mt. Kurama's cherry blossoms
have all fallen off.

Nawashiro ya Kurama no sakura chirinikeri

A flying kite
as in the sky yesterday
is still up there.

Ikanobori kino no sora no aridokoro

Ploughing the earth—
not even a singing bird
in the mountain's shadow.

Hata utsu ya tori sae nakanu yamakage ni

At Basho's Grass Hut
Ploughing a field!
Though the clouds did not move
they have gone.

(Basho-an e)
Hata utsu ya ugokanu kumo mo nakunarinu

In the Bamboo Hedge
An *uguisu*
moving about here and there
between small houses.

(Riraku)
Uguisu no achiokochi to suruya koie gachi

Uguisu sing
from far away all day long,
a farmer in his field.

Uguisu ni hinemosu toshi hata no hito

An *uguisu*
singing with its tiny
mouth wide open.

Uguisu no nakuya chiisaki kuchi aite

An *uguisu's*
voice in the distance all day,
now darkening.

Uguisu no koe toki hi mo kurenikeri

An *uguisu*—
while the family sits together
for rice eating time.

Uguisu ya kanai sorote meshi jibun

Onto the Otsu-painting
droppings fall with the passing
of a swallow.

Otsue ni fun otoshiyuku tsubame kana

Along Yamoto's roads
on shrines and on straw-thatched roofs
the swallows!

Yamatoji no miya mo waraya mo tsubame kana

Fluttering
it leaves the gold-screened room,
a swallow!

Futameite kin no ma o deru tsubame kana

With a shot pheasant,
going back home on the path,
the sun still high.

Kiji uchite kaeru ieji no hi wa takashi

With the geese gone
the field by the gate seems
more distant now.

Kari yukite kadota mo toku omowaruru

Young *ayu* fish and
with them, from the valley's bamboo,
one leaf floating by.

Wakaayu ya tani no ozasa mo hitoha yuku

While swimming
it wavers unsteadily,
the frog!

Oyogu toki yorubenaki sama no kawazu kana

While I pause to rest
they are heard from far off—
frogs!

Tatazumeba tokumo kikoyu kawazu kana

Nothing actual,
the feeling of holding in my fingers
a butterfly.

Utsutsunaki tsumami gokoro no kocho kana

The ambushed—
perched on his armor neckplates,
a butterfly!

Fusezei no shikoro ni tomaru kocho kana

On the hanging bell,
staying while he sleeps,
a butterfly!

Tsurigane ni tomarite nemuru kocho kana

The red plum's
fallen flowers seem to be burning
on the horse's droppings.

Kobai no rakka moyuran uma no fun

Early Spring
With white plum blossoms
these nights to the faint light of dawn
are turning.

(Shoshun)
Shiraume ni akuru yo bakari to narinikeri

Grass Hut
Two flower branches
of plum, one early, one late,
oh deeply loved!

(Soan)
Futa moto no ume ni chisoku o aisu kana

Picking plum blossoms
and fretting at my wrinkled hand—
fragrance.

Ume orite shiwade ni kakotsu kaori kana

White plum flowers!
The fragrance of an inkstone
in the Chinese guesthouse.

Hakubai ya sumi kanbashiki korokan

White blooming plum tree—
since whose time has it been there
just outside the hedge?

Shiraume ya taga mukashi yori kaki no soto

In the corners of the room
coldness lingers.
The plum flowers.

Sumi-zumi ni nokoru samusa ya ume no hana

Plum flowers blooming—
buying sashes, the Muro
courtesans!

Ume saite obi kau Muro no yujo kana

No lights on
for whoever lives there;
a house with plum blossoms.

Hi o okade hito aru sama ya ume no yado

Plum flowers far and near.
Shall I go to the south?
Shall I go north?

Ume ochi-kochi minami subeku kita subeku

Into water fell
its blossoms and disappeared,
plum tree on the shore.

Mizu ni chirite hana nakunarinu kishi no ume

Plum blossom essence
ascending higher—
the moon's halo.

Ume ga ka no tachinoborite ya tsuki no kasa

Instead of with cherry blossoms
with peach blossoms it seems most intimate,
the small house!

Sakura yori momo ni shitashiki koie kana

Flowers of the pear—
reading a letter by moonlight,
a woman.

Nashi no hana tsuki ni fumi yomu anna ari

Into an old well's
darkness falls
a camellia!

Furuido no kuraki ni otsuru tsubaki kana

A camellia falls,
and the rain of yesterday
spilling out.

Tsubaki ochite kino no ame o koboshi keri

Cherry blossoms darkening,
and far away from my home
on a path through fields!

Hana ni kurete waga ie toki nomichi kana

They swallow the clouds
and spit out the blossoms—
Yoshino's mountains!

Kumo o nonde hana o hakunaru Yoshi no yama

Darkness on the blossoms—
back to Kyoto where I live
now I will return.

Hana ni kurenu waga sumu kyo ni kaen'nan

As the moon's light moves across to the west
the flower's shadow to the east
is treading!

Gekko nishi ni watareba kaei higashi ni ayumu kana

At Yoshino,
going along a shortcut path—
mountain cherry blossoms.

Miyoshino no chikamichi yukeba yamazakura

When down off the horse
the height of the cherry blossoms
can be realized.

Uma orite takane no sakura mitsuketari

With blossoms fallen
in spaces between the twigs a temple
has appeared.

Hana chirite konoma no tera to narinikeri

Below the mountains
a noise of rice being hulled—
and wisteria.

Yamamoto ni kome fumu oto ya fuji no hana

Spring View
Rape-seed flowers!
the moon in the east and
the sun in the west.

(Shunkei)
Nanohana ya tsuki wa higashi ni hi wa nishi ni

Rape-seed flowers!
A whale passes without stopping
and the sea has darkened.

Nanohana ya kujira mo yorazu umi kurenu

Rape flowers in bloom—
the home of the priest,
but I pass by.

Nonohana ya hoshi ga yado wa towade sugishi

Rape flowers,
and for a while at noon
the ocean's sound.

Nanohana ya hiru hitoshikiri umi no oto

An aged temple
and a clay pot tossed out
in the parsley patch.

Furudera ya horoku sutsuru seri no naka

(After an outdoor cremation.)
The bone gatherer,
to him so very familiar
the violets.

Kotsu hirou hito ni shitashiki sumire kana

On my coming back,
how many pathways are there
through the spring grasses?

Waga kaeru michi ikusuji zo haru no kusa

On a bent hook
hangs an official's cap,
the lodging house in spring.

Orekugi ni eboshi kaketari haru no yado

Iris growing—
is it a pond? Five feet of
springtime's height.

Ayame ou ike go-shaku no haru fukashi

SUMMER

Although for about fifteen years Buson was in the Tokyo area and the northeast, as well as several times in Shikoku, most of his life was spent in Kansai, a west-central part of Japan, in places now called Suma Beach, Kobe, Osaka, Kyoto, and Tango Hanto (where Ama-no-Hashidate and Miyazu are). The weather patterns of Kansai are quite regular and persons living there are submerged in them despite present-day air conditioning in large buildings of concrete and plastic. Summer begins with spring showers gradually becoming early summer rains. Some days are fresh and cool; some steamy hot, so that everyone feels languorous and long afternoon naps are common whenever possible. Several times in this season the rains are apt to be heavy enough to cause some flooding and landslides. Closed-up rooms may become mouldy, and mildew attacks unprotected garments and stored possessions.

The shortness of summer night is given along with such images as dewdrops on a caterpillar, a beach fire left before it has finished burning, and a river boat trip where, at one town, the houses are seen closed up for the night and where, at another town when passed, windows are already being opened and daytime activity beginning.

Thoughtful appreciation can be felt in the persimmon flower being scooped up from a shallow well, a shower going over the eaves, or the moon's reflection on a river. The unpleasantness of the time of humid heat is conveyed by the image of a house seeming too crowded when it must be shared with a family, or by such images as flies, a cranky priest, sickness, having to labor, a coffin, insanity, and mosquitoes; however, the excited chicken on the roof shows us this time with humor. Anything hinting at coolness becomes pleasurable, such as a river or a bells' sound. It is not necessary to have lived in Japan to recognize the early summer rain poems, nor those of moonlight or streams.

The fresh new leaves of summer are abundant after warmth and rains. In most places in central Japan vegetation does not turn yellow or brown in summer, and the foliage becomes impenetrably thick. Buson's peonies are presumably cultivated ones and, sometimes, he writes of them in an ornate or Chinese way. He also tells of finding the flowering thorn or small wild roses, by pathways, where roads have ended, and while climbing a hill. This contrast between exotic and almost weedlike flowers shows something of the breadth of his responsive seeing. Both the small weeds and the exotic flowers are present in his environment, and he notes all. In the last few of the summer poems given here, there are flowers that bloom in difficult situations and a priest who must decide whether or not to pick one of them.

SUMMER HAIKU

At the shrine maidens' street
ceremonial robes being washed—
early summer.

Mikomachi ni yoki kinu sumasu uzuki kana

The night is brief—
on a hairy caterpillar
jewels of dew.

Mijikayo ya kemushi no ue ni tsuyu no tama

Brevity of the night—
where waves come beating in,
an abandoned fire.

Mijikayo ya namiuchigiwa no sutekagari

[*A boat trip.*]
The night is brief—
at Fushimi the doors are closed,
at Yodo windows opened.

Majikayo ya Fushimi no toboso Yodo no mado

A short night—
from a shallow well
scooping up a persimmon flower.

Mijika yo ya asai ni kaki no hana o kumu

In the short night
a passing shower
across the wooden eaves.

Mijika yo ya murasame wataru itabisashi

The night is brief—
on river shallows remains
a piece of the moon.

Mijikayo ya asase ni nokoru mizu no tsuki

On the veranda
to escape wife and children
How hot it is!

Hashii shite tsumako o sakuru atsusa kana

From the sick man's shoulder
a fly being brushed away—
the heat.

Byonin no kata no hae ou atsusa kana

A farmer
continuing to work—
the heat!

Hyakusho no ikite hataraku atsusa kana

A coolness—
lengthwise through the capital,
the flowing river

Suzushisa ya miyako o tate ni nagare gawa

Coolness—
separating from the bell,
the bell's voice.

Suzushisa ya kane o hanaruru kane no koe

Early-wheat harvest time—
the coffin of an itinerant priest
has just been carried by.

Mugiaki ya yugyo no hitsugi tori keri

The time of harvesting early-wheat
and loneliness on the face
of an insane woman!

Mugi no aki sabishiki kao no kyojo kana

A sick man's
palanquin is carried by
at the time of harvesting early-wheat.

Byonin no kago mo sugikeri mugi no aki

Early-wheat harvest time—
what is it that has frightened
the chicken on the roof?

Mugiaki ya nani ni odoroku yane no tori.

Even floating plants
almost being pushed under
in the summer rains.

Ukikusa mo shizumu-bakari you satsukiame

On the shortcut path,
stepping through water to cross
in the summer rains.

Chikamichi ya mizu fumi-wataru satsukiame

In early summer rain
it has become invisible,
the little path.

Samidare ni miezu narinuru komichi kana

Early summer rain—
thrusting into the azure sea
muddy river water.

Samidare ya aoumi o tsuku nigori mizu

Early summer rain—
a coin trodden on in the water
inside the ferry boat.

Samidare ya mizu ni zeni fumu watashibune

Early summer rain—
just when the lanterns of Kibune Shrine
have been extinguished.

Samidare ya Kibune no shato kiyuru toki

Early summer rains—
crossing the Oi River,
an accomplishment!

Samidare no Oi koshitaru kashikosa yo

Early summer rain—
facing toward the big river,
houses, two of them.

Samidare ya taiga o maeni ie niken

The rainy season—
bean vines clambering over
the carpenter's shed.

Samidare ya imo hai-kakaru daikugoya

The rainy season,
and the river with no name
a frightening thing.

Samidare ya no mo naki kawa no osoroshiki

An evening shower!
Holding onto the bushes,
a flock of sparrows.

Yudachi ya kusaba o tsukamu murasuzume

As they let in water at night,
voices of the paddy farmers—
a summer moon.

Yomizu toru satobito no koe ya natsu no tsuki

A temple watchman
stared vaguely at the grasses—
a summer moon.

Domori no ogusa nagametsu natsu no tsuki.

Unable to sleep,
going out from the cottage—
the summer moon.

Negurushiki fuse yo o dereba natsu no tsuki

Evading the fishnet,
and evading the fishing ropes,
the moon on the water.

Ami o more tsuna o more-tsutus mizu no tsuki

The place of putting down
the shoulder basket in the earthquake—
a summer field!

Oroshioku oi ni nae furu natsuno kana

At a Place Called Kaya in Tanba
A summer river
being crossed, how pleasing!
Sandals in my hands.

(Tanba no Kaya to-iu tokoro nite)
Natsu kawa o kosu ureshisa you te ni zori

The mountain stonecutter's
chisel is being cooled
in the clear water!

Ishikiri no nomi hiyashitaru shimizu kana

Where the rivers meet
there seems to be a quietness—
the clear water.

Ochi ote oto nakunareru shimizu kana

With two people
scooping it up, muddiness
comes to the clear water.

Futari shite musubeba nigoru shimizu kana

Rainfall on the grasses
just after the festival cart
passed by.

Kusa no ame matsuri no kuruma sugite nochi

A bad tempered priest
spilling from the bag as he walks
the rice donation!

Hara-ashiki so koboshiyuku semai kana

A View
Time of summer clothes,
and someone on the path through the field,
showing faintly white.

(Chobo)
Koromogae noji no hito hatsukani shiroshi

On shins of thin legs
breezes touching the hair—
time of summer clothes.

Yasezune no ke ni bifu ari koromogae

As it flared up,
the shyness of their faces—
mosquito punk!*

Moetachite kao hazukashiki kayari kana

With mosquito punk
the shelter becomes delightful—
moonlight on the grass.

Kayari shite yadori ureshi ya kusa no tsuki

*Punk is Chinese incense used to drive off bugs.

Lodging a priest tonight,
how happily the mosquito net
is being hung up.

So tomete ureshi to Kaya o tako tsuru

Hanging the mosquito net,
I shall make a jade mountain
inside my house.

Kaya tsurite suibi tsukuran ie no uchi

An evening breeze
tosses onto my face
one edge of the net.

Yukaze ya hito-ami kao e Kaya no suso

Signaling for the ferry boat,
showing above the wild grasses,
a fan.

Watashi yobu kusa no anata no ogi kana

To my eyes it is delightful—
the fan of my beloved,
completely white.

Me ni ureshi koigimi no ogi mashiro naru

Just to amuse myself
I will paint on the flat fan
with juice of grasses.

Tesusabi no uchiwa egakan kusa no shiru

A hanging sachet bag—
the bathing woman behind the curtain
touched by the wind.

Kakego ya makuyu no kimi ni kaze sawaru

My own shadow
trodden on in the shallows—
cooling off.

Waga kage o asase ni funde suzumi kana

It is dawn.
Fish that evaded the cormorants
swim in the shallows.

Shinonome ya u o nogaretaru io asashi

Spirits of the dead
often flying over at night,
the cormorant-fishing river.

Naki tama no tobu yo mama aru ukawa kana

Wolves do not come closer
to the fire of the hunters
until it dies down.

Okami wa yoraji hogushi no kiyuru made

Wind from the mountains
caresses the young rice plants
as it passes by.

Yamaoroshi sanae o nadete yuku e kana

The divorced wife too,
she must step into his field
for rice transplanting!

Sararetaru mi o fumikonde taue kana

The conch shell blown at noon,
songs of workers in the rice fields
no longer heard.

Uma no kai tauta oto naku narinikeri

From deep water
the sound of a sharp sickle
cutting water reeds.

Mizu fukaku toki kama narasu makomogari

The sushi lunch box,
while washing it in the shallows,
playful drifting fish!

Sushioke o araeba asaki yugyo kana

Hototogisu
over the Heian castle town
flying aslant.

Hototogisu Heianjo o sujikaini

In evening wind—
water is slapping against
legs of a blue heron.

Yukaze ya mizu aosagi no hagi o utsu

A bat flying!
The wife across from my house
looks in my direction.

Kawahori ya mukai no nyobo kochi o miru

He presents *ayu*
then goes on without visiting—
the gateway at midnight.

Ayu kurete yorade sugiyuku yowa no kado

I grasp
in the darkness of the heart
a firefly.

Tsukamitorite kokoro no yami no hotaru kana

At a wayside shrine,
burning before the Buddha,
a firefly!

Tsujido no hotoke ni tomosu hotaru kana

An old well!
Jumping at a mosquito, a fish's
sound of darkness.

Furuido ya ka ni tobu uo no oto kurashi

Mosquitoes humming
each time a honeysuckle flower
falls from the vine.

Ka no koe su nindo no hana no chiru tabi ni

Far and near, far and near
sound of cascading waters—
the fresh new leaves!

Ochi-kochi ni taki no oto kiku wakaba kana

On the valley trail
a person walking looks small—
fresh new leaves!

Taniji yuku hito wa chiisaki wakaba kana

By the shallow river,
to the west and to the east—
fresh new leaves!

Asakawa no nishi-shi higashi -su wakaba kana

Beside the mountain
a boat being rowed—
the fresh new leaves.

Yama ni soute kobune kogiyuku wakaba kana

Only Mt. Fuji
is not covered with them—
fresh new leaves.

Fuji hitotsu uzumi-nokoshite wakaba kana

On a hilltop
the firm-standing castle,
and fresh new leaves.

Zetcho no shiro tanomoshiki wakaba kana

Coming to see them again
in the evening, blossoms
have become fruit.

Kitemireba yube no sakura mi to narinu

Young bamboo!
At Hashimoto, the harlot,
is she still there?

Wakatake ya Hashimoto no yujo ariyanashi

A peony fallen—
on top of one another
two petals, three petals.

Botan chirite uchikasanarinu nisan pen

After cutting the peony
my mind seems emptied—
twilight.

Botan kitte ki no otoroishi yube kana

The golden screen,
how it glitters!
The peony!

Kinpei no kakuyaku to-shite botan kana

A mountain ant,
it is plainly seen
on a white peony.

Yamaari no akarasamanari hakubotan

For a hundred leagues,
rain clouds forbidden to come—
the peonies!

Ho hyaku-ri amagumo yosenu botan kana

After it has fallen
its image still stands—
the peony flower.

Chirite nochi omokage ni tatsu botan kana

In the quietness
of a lull between visitors,
the peony flower!

Seki toshite kyaku no taema no botan kana

The weighty cart's
resounding vibration.
The peony trembling.

Jiguruma no todoro to hibiku botan kana

An iris
with a hawk's droppings
splashed over.

Kakitsubata betarito tobi no taretekeru

Ascending the Eastern Slope
Flowering thorn—
the path by my home village
is like this!

(Kano toko ni noboreba)
Kana-ibara kokyo no michi ni nitaru kana

The road has ended,
close fragrance of blooming
thorn bushes!

Michi taete ka ni semarisaku ibara kana

Feeling melancholy
while climbing the hill,
flowering thorn.

Ureitsutsu oka ni noboreba hana-ibara

A white lotus,
and pondering whether to cut it—
the priest's dilemma.

Byakuren o kiran tozo omou so no sama

Yellow pond-lilies,
two clumps of them blooming
in the rain.

Kohone no futamoto saku ya ame no naka

By a roadside
the pulled-up duckweed flowered
in early evening rain.

Michinobe n o karumo hanasaku yoi no ame

By lightning
the small house was burned down
and now melon flowers!

Kaminari ni koie wa yakarete uri no hana

AUTUMN

Autumn is the best season in central Japan: typhoons soon stop threatening, storms are few, heat lessens, air becomes drier, everyone feels more vigorous, and actually a whole series of autumn flowers begins to bloom in fields and forests. The greenness continues, though much of the foliage among the evergreens, shrubs, and trees very gradually changes to red, vermillion, and gold. There is sunshine most days, and the coldness comes so slowly that it may scarcely be noted before December. Snow falls earlier in the mountains, but in the valleys and towns of Kansai, flowers and vegetables are still growing. There is little wind; people are inclined to move about busily in their work and go on occasional excursions for sightseeing amid the bright maple leaves. Varieties of crickets sound incessantly.

> The cold penetrates
> while in the stream of Yokawa
> clothes are being rinsed.

As nights become cold in unheated houses, there is a growing awareness of the chill, and apparently, Buson knew what it was to have a cold with sneezing and a dripping nose. Too, late autumn seems often to bring a feeling of loneliness and mild melancholy, which can be found throughout Japanese literature. Buson expresses this, sometimes only vaguely, in a number of pieces; seemingly, his loneliness is not acute. One haiku says that being alone may be pleasant too; in another, he feels strengthened by reading a sutra; and the moon is recognized as a friend by someone who is lonely.

Creatures of autumn include crows, rats, pheasants, geese, horses, deer, rabbits, dragonflies, and fish. The moon seems to be the most beautiful sight of autumn, and in combinations with various locations—a shabby village street, Lake Suwa, on a ridge, Hirosawa Pond—it is associated with loneliness. Especially exquisite are poems about dewdrops—on a hunter's chest, on a warrior's bow, on wild rose thorns, on a huntsman's quiver. As with many of the subjects of haiku, dew has long been used in Japanese poetry. The eighth century poetry collection the *Manyoshu* has poems in which it appears, as do many of the other subjects that are constantly used in haiku. Whether or not Buson intended readers to be aware of the ancient poems and later ones, as well as Chinese poems, or whether he wrote of the same images for the simple reason that he himself experienced them, does not matter. Dewdrops, moonlight, rats—they are all still on the earth and can be directly experienced. A deer crying out was another image used for autumn loneliness in Japanese poetry since ancient times, though today such a sound is rarely heard.

For autumn, Buson also wrote of the young boys who assist a priest, do odd jobs at a temple, and may eventually become monks or priests themselves. We see one such boy walking on the golden leaves fallen from a ginkgo tree perhaps fifty feet tall in a silent and deserted mountainside forest. Some philosophic feeling may also be present here for the child who will perhaps spend his life isolated with

Buddhism. The haiku in which another such boy is gathering acorns in his free time may be showing him as a child who is lonely and attempting to amuse himself; or who is happily playing thus; or who is performing yet another task required by a strict master. If a non-Japanese interprets differently than a Japanese, this does not detract from the haiku. We see these boys as we might if we were the passerby, aware of them for only the moment they are within our sight. Questions about them remain unanswered, but they were seen and their existence acknowledged; perhaps, this brief and unimportant scene has a hint of poignancy that is not sentiment and contains a Buddhist attitude.

Among the flowers common to autumn, the most renowned are chrysanthemums—written of here as an intimate flower persistently clinging to village dooryards. They may still be seen today, even in front of great, collapsed, grass-roofed houses in long deserted mountain villages. They go on blooming by themselves even after man has left them. Japanese are also fond of bush clover (J. *hagi*; L. *lespedeza*), a shrub with minute pinkish flowers that drop off even more quickly than cherry blossoms. Several varieties of small autumn orchids can be found along mountain paths and in fields surrounded by forests. Some simple kinds are grown in gardens too, and in Buson's poem, the one seen at night is probably of the latter variety. Morning glories (*asagao, yugao, hirugao*, moon flowers, evening glories, convolvulus, bindweed) are profuse from midsummer until the nights become too cold. They grow wild in tangles along embankments and everywhere, even on seashore sand, continuously flowering in white and pink. Larger, colorful blooms are cultivated in gardens, often in rows of pots with a network of stakes and strings for them to climb. Even the most shabby of slum houses may have the large blue flowers planted along one wall. We find them mentioned throughout Japanese poetry, tales and essays, as are all the most popular plants. In such a small insular land, everywhere divided by walls of mountains or the sea, where rice culture and the society routinized life, such scenic details were warmly recognized and were part of the rich culture portrayed in an art and writing where formalization increased awareness of the qualities of the fauna and even made a simple daily seeing emotionally satisfying.

The plumed pampas grass is another very significant plant, not only for its graceful beauty, and because it can be found on deserted windswept high places where the sky is wide and autumn and winter come early, as death comes early to some, but for previous literary associations also. When the plumes are gone, the withered grasses on a moor being swept by the wind represent the most desolate and sometimes passionately sad of scenes—a sort of King Lear mood, or the emotion in the death-piece of Basho. Buson's haiku on a crow would also recall to most Japanese one by Basho on the same subject.

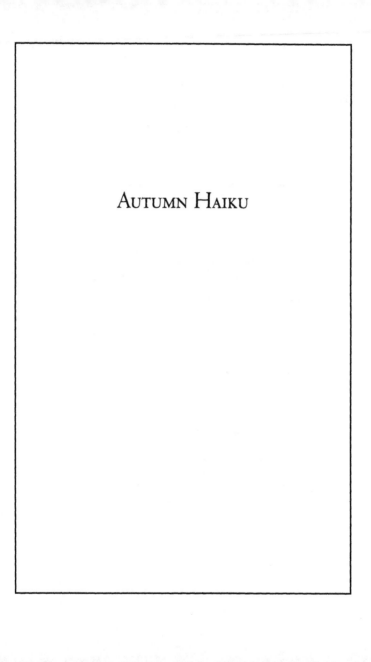

Autumn Haiku

That autumn has come
must be admitted—
a sneeze!

Aki kinu to gaten sasetaru kusame kana

The first day of autumn!
Simple hot water to drink but fragrant
at the temple hospital.

Aki tatsu ya sayu kobashiki seyakuin

At the bottom of the hot spring
my feet are visible
this autumn morning.

Yu no soko ni waga ashi miyuru kesa no aki

The cold penetrates
while in the stream of Yokawa
clothes are being rinsed.

Mi ni shimu ya Yokawa no kinu o sumasu toki

It goes into me—
the comb of my long gone wife,
to step on it in the bedroom.

Mi ni shimu ya naki tsuma no kushi o neya ni fumu

Going to See a Mountain Friend
Enroute to the monkey king
on a cold night,
a visiting rabbit.

(Yamaga ni Yadoru)
Sarudono no yosamu toiyuku usagi kana

Thinner and thinner
the moon as it diminishes—
a cold night!

Kakekakete tsuki mo nakunaru yosamu kana

With lantern in hand,
taking out a heavy quilt—
a cold night!

Teshoku shite yoki futon dasu yosamu kana

The other side of the wall
a rattling of things—
a cold night!

Kabedorari mono gototsukasu yosamu kana

A cricket crawls up
the kettle hook over the hearth—
a cold night.

Kirigirisu jizai o noboru yosamu kana

With nose adrip,
alone at a game of *go*—
a cold night!

Hana tarete hitori go o ustu yosamu kana

A penniless priest
carving an image of Buddha—
a cold night!

Hinso no Hotoke o kizamu yosamu kana

Autumn dusk—
turned into a Buddha image,
a badger!

Aki no kure hotoke ni bakeru tanuki kana

A Feeling of Aging
Compared to last year,
this has been even more loneliness—
autumn evening.

(Rokai)
Kyonen yori mata sabishii zo aki no kure

Looking away from me
stands a long-billed snipe;
autumn twilight.

Achira-muki ni shigi mo tachi tari aki no kure

Going through the gate,
I also am a wanderer
this twilight in autumn.

Mon o dereba ware mo yuku-hito aki no kure

In my loneliness
my cane has been left somewhere,
an evening in autumn.

Sabishi-mi ni tsue wasuretari aki no kure

In autumn dusk
at the wayside shrine for the Jizo image
I pour more votive oil.

Aki no kure tsuji no jizo ni abura sasu

Being alone
may also be pleasant—
autumn dusk.

Sabishisa no ureshiku mo ari aki no kure

Reading a sutra
I feel strengthened;
autumn dusk.

Kundoku no kyo o yosuga ya aki no kure

Coming alone
to visit someone who is alone
in the autumn dusk.

Hitori kite hitori o tou ya aki no kure

My life will end,
but still it has times of leisure—
autumn dusk.

Kagiri aru inochi no hima ya aki no kure

Going out the gate,
happening to meet an old acquaintance
this twilight in autumn.

Mon o dete kojin ni ainu aki no kure

Ending their flight
one by one, crows in the
autumn dusk.

Tobi-tsukusu karasu hitotsu-zutsu aki no kure

The rat's children
crying out squeak, squeak—
autumn midnight.

Ko-nezumi no chichiyo to naku ya yowa no aki

Autumn night—
reading an old book,
the Nara priest.

Aki no yo ya furuki fumi yomu Nara-hoshi

Asleep in the shelter of eaves,
he is chased away by a voice—
autumn midnight.

Noki ni neru hito ou koe ya yowa no aki

A mountain pheasant
moves his feet on the branch—
the long night!

Yamadori no eda fumikayuru yonaga kana

A small amount,
the debt I was asked to pay
at the end of autumn.

Isasaka-na oime kowarenu kure no aki

No trail to follow
where the teacher has wandered off—
the end of autumn.

Ato kakusu shi no yukigata ya kure no aki

At Basho's Grass Hut
Almost winter,
and the cloudiness of a shower
where it begins from.

(Rakuto Basho-an nite)
Fuyu chikashi shigure no kumo mo koko yori zo

Even more so
because of being alone
the moon is a friend.

Nakanaka ni hitori areba zo tsuki o tomo

Moon in the sky's center,
shabbiness on the village street—
just passing through.

Tsuki tenshin mazushiki machi o tori keri

The boat for viewing the moon,
and my tobacco pipe fallen—
the shallow water!

Tsukimi-bune kiseru o otosu asase kana

In harvest moonlight—
rabbits seem to be running over
the Lake of Suwa.

Meigetsu ya usagi no wataru Suwa no umi

A full moon!
At night no one is staying
in the tea-stall on the ridge.

Meigetsu ya yoru wa hito sumanu mine no chaya

A full moon!
In the Sacred Fountain Garden
a fish is dancing.

Meigetsu ya Shinsen-en no io odoru

Hirosawa Pond
With water dried up,
the pond is misshapen!
Late autumn moon.

(Hirosawa)
Mizu karete ike no hizumi ya nochinotsuki

A sazanka tree's
open spaces are revealed,
late autumn moon.

Sazanka no konoma misekeri nochinotsuki

White dewdrops!
Enough to dampen the hair
on the hunter's chest.

Shiratsuyu ya satsuo no munage nururu hodo

The warrior
continues on, brushing off dewdrops
with the end of his bow!

Mononofu no tsuyu haraiyuku yuhazu hana

White drops of dew
on spines of the thornbush,
one for each!

Shiratsuyu ya ibara no hari ni hitotsuzutsu

The hunting grounds'
dewdrops making heavy
the quiver!

Karikura no tsiuyu ni omotaki utsubo kana

A taker of human lives,
is it deep water over there
in the fog?

Hito o toru fuchi wa kashiko ka kiri no naka

While feeling sad—
a fishing line being blown
by the autumn wind.

Kanashisa ya tsuri no ito fuku aki no kaze

Autumn wind,
and small fish have been strung up to dry
from the eaves of a beach house.

Akikaze ya hiuo kaketaru hamabisashi

Autumn wind—
reciting poems in the wine shop,
fishermen and woodcutters.

Aki kaze ya shushi ni shi utau gyosha shosha

To the castle of Toba
five or six horses hurrying
in the autumn storm.

Toba-dono e go-rokki isogu nowaki kana

The visiting priest
comes down from the upstairs room—
the autumn storm!

Kyakuso no nikai orikuru nowaki kana

After the autumn storm,
lamplight from a doorway
at the village edge.

Nowaki yande to ni hi no moruru mura hazure

The bottomless
pail tumbles and walks around
in the autumn storm.

Soko no nai oke koke-aruku nowaki kana

With the lightning,
a sound of dripping down!
Dew on the bamboo.

Inazuma ni koboruru oto ya take no tsuyu

Lightning!
Waves of the sea encircling
these "Islands of Autumn."

Inazuma ya nami mote yueru akitsushima

With the pine torch out
the sea is dimly visible—
a field of flowers!

Matsu keshite umi sukoshi miyuru hanano kana

By the high tide
swept away so they swim upstream,
the tiny fish!

Hatsushio ni owarete noboru kouo kana

On just four or five people,
moonlight shining down—
oh, their dancing!

Shigonin ni tsuki ochikakaru odori kana

To the nurse's
ears as the night grows late,
the folk-dancing!

Kanbyo no mimi ni fukeyuku odori kana

With the water dried-up
his thin legs are long—
a scarecrow in the rice field!

Mizu ochite hosohagi takaki hagashi kana

While cutting down the rice,
the little weeds with autumn
sunlight on them.

Ine kareba ogusa ni aki no hi no ataru

Far and near,
and far and near, the sound
of cloth-pounding.

Ochikochi ochikochi to utsu kinuta kana

A deer in the cold,
his horns pressed close to his body
like withered twigs.

Shika samushi tsuno mo mi ni sou kareki kana

Three times it cried out
but now not heard anymore,
a deer in the rain.

Mitabi naite kikoezu narinu shika no koe

Even over Kii Province,
without coming down at night, travels
a solitary goose.

Kinoji nimo orizu yo o yuku Kari hitotsu

A small bird comes;
the sound, how delightful
by the wooden eaves.

Kotori kuru oto ureshisa yo itabisashi

[Visiting Uji in autumn.]
The *ayu* have gone downstream
and higher and higher
the mountain ridges!

Ayu ochite iyoiyo takaki onoe kana

Sunlight aslant
at the border gate, and on the spears
dragonflies!

Hi wa naname sekiya no yari ni tonbo kana

The dragonflies
of my beloved village,
the color of the walls!

Tonbo ya mura natsukashiki kabe no iro

Treading on ginko leaves,
a priest's boy quietly
going down the mountain!

Icho funde shizukani chigo no gezan kana

At Takao
Poet Saigyo's
bedcovers have appeared—
maple leaves!

(Takao)
Saigyo no yagu mo dete aru momiji kana

The mountain darkening
and the redness of the maples
taken away.

Yama kurete momiji no ake o ubai keri

Girls from Ohara,
the hastiness of their feet!
Maples at evening.

Oharame no ashi no hayasa yo yu-momiji

White chrysanthemums
growing abundantly in the yard
and on to the farm field.

Shiragiku ya niwa ni amarite hatake made

A village of a hundred houses
and not even a single gate
without chrysanthemums.

Mura hyaku-ko kiku naki kado mo mienu kana

The little fox,
what made him cough—
in a field with bush clover?

Kogitsune no nani ni musekemu kohagihara

A difficult journey—
raindrops on sagging bush clover
trodden upon.

Uki tabi ya hagi no shizue no ame o fumu

An orchid at night—
hidden by its own fragrance,
the white flower.

Yoru no ran ka ni kakurete ya hana shiroshi

Morning glory!
One flower deep with
the color of water's deepness.

Asagao ya ichirin fukaki fuchi no iro

Morning glories—
the indigo color on the towel's edge
no longer satisfies me.

Asagao ya tenugui no hashi no ai o kakotsu

Mountains have darkened,
and the field, in a twilight
with pampas grass!

Yama wa kurete no wa tasogare no susuki kana

In wind that pushes,
cutting the pampas grass
is an old man!

Oikaze ni susuki karitoru okina kana

Picking up acorns,
the temple boy of Yokawa
in his hour of leisure.

Shii hirou yokawa no chigo no itoma kana

Gleaning the grains that fell,
following the sunlight,
they move along.

Ochibo hiroi hi ataru ho e ayumiyuku

They look beautiful
after the autumn storm,
the red peppers.

Utsukushi ya nowaki no ato no togarashi

Parting from a Friend
Following Kiso Road
I shall become aged
alone in autumn.

(Kojin ni wakaru)
Kiso-ji yukite iza toshi-yoran aki hitori

The autumn lanterns!
How alluring Nara's
street-sales fair.

Aki no hi ya yukashiki Nara no dogu ichi

The candlewick's
thinness is all there is.
Autumn hermitage.

Toshin no hosoki yousuga ya aki no io

The highway robber
now a disciple with shaven head
on an autumn journey.

Oihagi o deshi ni sorikeri aki no tabi

Autumn boredom—
yet this evening will be remembered
by tomorrow.

Mi no aki ya koyoi o shinobu asu mo ari

At Suma Temple
With sounds of a flute
the close approach of waves at
Suma in autumn.

(Suma-dera nite)
Fue no ne ni nami mo yori-kuru Suma no aki

Somehow in autumn
azaleas flowering in
a Shiga village.

Aki tamatama tsutsuji hana-saku Shiga no sato

This evening a crow
of autumn melancholy
speaks out.

Yugarasu aki no aware o tsugenikeri

WINTER

Although the Kansai winter is mild, it is colder than in the more southern part of Japan, and an unheated house on a day without sunshine when a wind is blowing can be a discomfort, particularly when one is not active.

> Treading on the dishes,
> rats make a noise
> of coldness!

Layers of winter garments were worn, and the winter quilts were heavy. Tiny pots or cases containing live coals kept fingers from numbing. Farmhouses had a sunken wood-burning hearth in the middle of a large room that served as the kitchen and family room. Some rooms had a square, sunken hearth about a yard wide with space for the feet of those sitting on four sides as well as a charcoal firepot covered over with a low table that had a quilt spread on a frame just under its top and extending over the laps of those sitting around it. This *kotatsu* is still common, now usually heated by electricity. It is used for meals, study, family talk while doing small tasks, and entertaining. In fact, all sedentary daily life centers around it. Staying in such a position, feet toasting all day and the back exposed to whatever winter breezes penetrated through cracks and sliding paper panels, could produce stiffness and rheumatic aches, but it did allow for an informal intimacy between those within a house, as did the steaming hot baths, often communal, that warmed the body thoroughly.

The winter haiku give us glimpses of the season, inside

the house and outside. We can get a feeling of age and puttering, low vitality and a withdrawnnes —a great contrast to the sensuous outgoing poems of spring and summer. Even the water birds have gone. The Buddha image is presented as a possible source or fuel for a little warmth, an old Zen concept. The rice offering before the Buddha is stale and cold, neglected—not like the summer haiku where a firefly is seen shining before the Buddha. Hungry birds and rats seek food. The moon of winter is presented as austere, even when beautiful. Thoughts about Basho seem melancholy. Snow and nipping winds isolate and make a home necessary. Buson is aware of suffering: the poor, a hooked fish, a stumbling horse, the sound of windblown water, a lone peddler, his own bones, the freezing streams, a bird being eaten, a woman at her cold work, a lowly priest, the withered field, the dog that is cold.

But winter is brief, and many days are sunlit enough for a wall of a room to be slid open to let the warm brightness penetrate fully inside. All winter, tea-bush flowers and the *sasanqua*, or other varieties of winter camellias, are white and pink on hedges and small trees. The first early plum blossoms and narcissus can be found in fragrant clumps in sheltered nooks. Today in Kyoto, the snowfall usually melts within a few hours, and the clear air is hardly freezing if one is moving about. Ice on ponds is generally gone by midday. Certainly, all is not desolate in this winter unless one is looking for images to support a severe or melancholy mood. The birdsong of the *uguisu* can sometimes be heard while there is

WINTER HAIKU

Early winter—
I thought I was going visiting
but the person has come here.

Hatsu fuyu ya towan to omau hito kimasu

In the aging house,
the crooked door being straightened,
a spring-like winter day.

Furuie no yugami o naosu koharu kana

Treading on the dishes,
rats make a noise
of coldness!

Sara o fumu nezumi no oto no samusa kana

Neglected, the old offering
of rice to the Buddha image,
how cold it is!

Wasure-oku hotoke no meshi no samusa kana

Into the deep well
drops the thin edging of ice—
cold!

I no moto e usuba o otosu samusa kana

To strike the temple bell,
I go out from my bed-quilts—
the cold!

Kane tsuki ni yogi o hanaruru samusa kana

Not even water birds
seen while I cross the inlet,
such coldness.

Mizudori mo mienu e wataru samusa kana

A handsaw
sounding like poverty
at midnight in winter.

Nokogiri no oto mazushisa you yowa no fuyu

In the Hida Mountains
the village pawnshop is closed—
a winter evening.

Hida-yama no shichiya tozashinu yowa no fuyu

A winter night!
The old image of the Buddha
should be the first thing burned.

Fuyu no yo ya furuki hotoke o mazu takan

Wearing a Woven Hat and Straw Sandals (from Basho)
Basho has gone
and ever since then
a year cannot end appropriately

(Kasa kite waraji hakinagara)
Basho satte sono nochi imada toshi kurezu

I shall go to bed—
New Year's Day is a matter
for tomorrow.

Izaya nen ganjitsu wa mata asu no koto

Winter bareness;
in the north shadow of the house,
cutting green onions.

Fuyuzare ya kita no yakage no nira o karu

Winter bareness—
little birds seeking food
in the patch of green onions.

Fuyuzare ya kotori no asaru nirabatake

In the Suburbs
Silence
in a field with oak trees.
The winter moon.

(Kogai)
Shizukanaru kashi no ki hara ya fuyu no tsuki

Changing into stone,
the top of the camphor tree!
The winter moon.

Ishi to naru kusu no kozue ya fuyu no tsuki

Under the winter moon
chopping up firewood,
the man of the temple!

Kangetsu ni ki o waru tera no otoko kana

A winter moon!
Happening to meet a priest
going over a bridge.

Kangetsu ya so ni ikiau hashi no ue

A winter moon!
Over the gateless temple
the sky's elevation.

Kangetsu ya mon naki tera no ten takashi

Winter moon!
Among the leafless trees
three bamboos.

Kangetsu ya kareki no naka no take sankan

Winter moon!
After a knocking at the gate,
the sound of shoes.

Kangetsu ya mon o tatakeba kutsu no oto

Winter moon!
Feeling the small pebbles
under my shoes.

Kangetsu ya koishi no sawaru kutsu no soko

The ferry boat,
and on one who just missed it
the first winter shower.

Hito-watashi okureta hito ni shigure kana

(For the death anniversary of Basho.)
With the soundlessness of winter rain
on mosses, vanished days
are remembered.

Shigure oto nakute koke ni mukashi o shinobu kana

Winter rainfall!
A rat runs across
the top of the koto

Shigururu ya nezumi no wataru koto no ue

Camphor tree roots
silently becoming wet
in a winter shower.

Kusu no ne o shizukani nurasu shigure kana

(At a memorial service for Basho.)
His straw raincoat and bamboo hat
convey an awareness of the master—
winter rain.

Mino-kasa no ihatsu tsutaete shigure kana

What is in front of my eyes
changes into a scene of the past—
a winter shower.

Me no mae ni mukashi o misuru shigure kana

Herons getting wet
while the cranes are still in sunlight—
a winter shower!

Sagi nurete tsuru ni hi no teru shigure kana

An old man's love,
while trying to forget it,
a winter rainfall.

Oi ga koi wasuren to sureba shigure kana

Carrying a saucepan
over a little bridge in Yodo,
someone in the snow.

Nabe sagete yodo no kobashi o yuki no hito

Snow in the evening,
the snipe seems to have
returned again.

Yuki no kure shigi wa modotte iru yona

No lodging offered
among the lanterns! In snow
the row of houses.

Yado kasanu hokage ya yuki no ie tsuzuki

Asking for a night's lodging,
the swords are thrown down—
a heavy snowstorm!

Yado kase to katana nagedasu fubuki kana

My own foolishness must be endured—
the window darkened
by snowy bamboo.

Gu ni taeyo to mado o kurosu yuki no take

A tethered horse
and snow on both of
the stirrups!

Tsunagi uma yuki isso no abumi kana

Snow snapping off twigs,
I hear it in the darkness
of the night.

Yukiore mo kikoete kuraki yo naru kana

A snowy morning
and smoke from the kitchen roof—
it is good.

Yuki no ashita omoya no keburi medetasa yo

In an old pond
a straw sandal half sunken—
wet snow!

Furuike ni zori shizumite mizore kana

A nipping wind!
How do they exist—
houses, five of them?

Kogarashi ya nani ni yo wataru ie goken

The nipping wind
blowing through its gills!
A hooked fish.

Kogarashi ni era fukaruru ya kagi no io

In a tree-withering wind
he stumbles suddenly—
the horse going home.

Kogarashi ya hita to tsumazuku modori uma

A nipping wind!
Tearing into the rock,
the voice of the water.

Kogarashi ya iwa ni sakeyuku mizu no koe

A nipping wind!
Reading characters cut into a stone,
a solitary priest.

Kogarashi ya ishibumi o yomu so hitori

Winter wind!
A charcoal peddler all alone
in a small ferry boat.

Kogarashi ya sumiuri hitori watashibune

Returning from Naniwa with Kito
Frost for a hundred leagues—
inside the boat I
monopolize the moon.

(Kito to Naniwa yori kaesa)
Shimo hyuakuri shuchu ni ware tsuki o ryosu

A dandelion
blooming out of season,
frost on the path.

Tanpopo no wasurebana ari michi no shimo

My bones
keep touching against the quilts
in the frosty night!

Waga hone no futon ni sawaru shimoyo kana

The mountain stream
brings less and less water—
frozen to ice!

Yamamizu no heru hodo herite kori kana

With exposed teeth
the ice on the writing brush
is bitten off tonight.

Ha arawani fude no kori o kamu yo kana

The river in winter!
In her boat, washing vegetables,
there is a woman.

Fuyu-kawa ya fune ni na o arau Onna ari

River in winter—
who left behind on the bank
a red turnip?

Fuyukawa ya ta ga hikisutete akakabura

A flying squirrel
devouring a small bird—
the withered field!

Musasabi no kotori hami-iru kareno kana

The high priest
relieves his noble bowels
in a desolate field.

Daitoko no kuso hiriowasu kareno kana

Quietly, weakly,
onto a rock the sunlight comes
in a withered field.

Shojo to-shite ishi ni hi no iru kare no kana

Not yet quite dark
but stars are shining—
the withered field!

Kuremadaki hoshi no kagayaku kareno kana

Saying goodby
to one who is going over the mountains—
the withered field.

Yama koyuru hito ni wakarete hare no kana

The season's holy chant
from the teapot too, "dabu, dabu"—
for ten nights.

Ana toto cha mo dabu-dabu to juya kana

The dog pressed to the door
rattles it as he turns in sleep—
the seclusion of winter.

To ni inu no negaeru oto ya fuyugomori

Going off to sleep,
I want to hide in myself—
winter isolation.

Ineburite ware ni kakuren fuyugomori

To the kitchen door
whose wife and children have come?
The seclusion of winter.

Katte made tare ga tsumako zo fuyugomori

When near the hem of my robe,
not near my heart—
the charcoal brazier.

Suso ni okite kokoro ni toki hioke kana

Coals under ashes—
just now starting to boil
the stuff in the pot.

Uzumibi ya tsuiniwa niyuru nabe no mono

The little baby's
bonnet far down on his eyebrows,
tender feelings.

Midorigo no zukin mabukaki itooshimi

Pull it up by my head,
or down to cover my feet—
the shabby quilt?

Kashira eya kaken suso eya furu-busuma

Where whale meat is sold,
the market's knives
resounding!

Kujira-uri ichi ni katana o narashikeri

Water birds!
Washing vegetables in a boat
there is a woman.

Mizudori ya fune ni na o arau Onna ari

Winter *uguisu*—
long ago in Wang-wei's
garden hedge too!

Fuyu uguisu mukashi Oi ga kakine kana

Uguisu!
What is that rustling?
Frost on the bushes.

Uguisu ya nani kosotsukasu yabu no shimo

A fox-fire and,
in a skull, rain has made
 a pool tonight.

Kitsunebi ya dokuro ni ame no tamaru yo ni

The narrow path
not completely covered
with fallen leaves.

Hosomichi o uzumimo yaranu ochiba kana

Weather from the west,
they pile up in the east—
the fallen leaves.

Nishi fukeba higashi ni tamaru ochiba kana

The expected person's
footsteps sounding from a distance
on fallen leaves.

Machibito no ashioto toki ochiba kana

A roof thatcher's
footsteps on the fallen leaves
above the bedroom.

Yane-fuki no ochiba fumu nari neya no ue

Following the Master's Poem
The old pond's
frog is becoming aged
in the fallen leaves.

(Soo no ku o osoite)
Furu-ike no kawazu oi-yuku ochiba kana

The tea-plant flowers—
whether white or whether yellow,
hard to tell.

Cha no hana ya shiro nimo ki nimo obotsukana

Tea bush flowers.
Coming out of a back gate,
a tofu peddler.

Cha no hana ya uramon e deru tofu-uri

The loquat blossoms,
even birds do not like them—
the day is ending.

Biwa no hana tori mo susamezu hi kuretari

Winter plum flowers,
the sound of their being broken off!
An aged elbow.

Kanbai o taoru habiki ya oi ga hizi

Wandering in Northern Kyoto
Mandarin ducks,
their beauty made apparent
in winter woods.

(Rakuhoku ni asobu)
Oshidori ni bi o tsukushite ya fuyu kodachi

When the axe cuts in,
surprise at the perfume—
woods in winter.

Ono irete ka ni odoroku ya fuyukodachi

Narcissus!
In the chilly capital,
some here, some there.

Suisne ya samuki miyako no koko kashiko

Narcissus
and a lovely woman
with a headache.

Suisen ya bijin kobe o itamurashi

Winter chrysanthemums—
When will their time of fullness come,
clusters of unopened buds?

Kangiku ya itsu o sakari no tsubomi gachi

Winter chrysanthemums,
in the village where the sunshine
comes to one corner.

Kangiku ya hi no teru mura no kartahotori

Concerning Basho, Kompukuji Temple
I too when dead
want to be near this stone marker—
the withered pampas grass.

(Konpukuji Basho-o-haka)
Ware mo shishite hi ni hotori sen kareobana

Withered pampas grass,
in the daytime winds
it is being blown!

Kareobana mahiru no kaze ni fukareiru

Withered grasses where
a fox messenger on flying legs
passed through.

Kusa karete kitsune no hikyaku tori keri

Buying leeks
and then between withered trees
having returned.

Negi kote kareki no naka o kaerikeri

The Three Long Poems

MOURNING FOR THE OLD POET HOKUJU
(Hokuju-rosen o Itamu)

You left in the morning, at evening my heart
is in a thousand pieces.
Why are you far away?

Thinking of you, I go to a hillside and wander.
Around the hillside, why such a sadness?

Dandelions yellow and shepherds-purse blooming white—
nobody to look.

I heard a pheasant call and call without stopping.
Once a friend was across the river, living.

Ghostly smoke rises up but with a strong west wind in fields
of small bamboo grasses and reedy fields
it cannot linger anywhere.

Once a friend was across the river, living, but today
not even the birds call out *hororo.*

You left in the morning, at evening my heart
is in a thousand pieces.
Why are you far away?

In my grass hut by the Amida image I light no candle
and offer no flowers. I sit here alone this evening
filled with homage.

Priest Buson
with a thousand bowings

This poem was first published long after the death of Buson. It might have been written
in 1745 when he was only twenty-nine, or perhaps much later.

SLOW-RIVER SONG, IN THREE PARTS
(Denga-Ka)

[The woman speaks, in the style of a Chinese poem.]

Spring water with plum blossom petals afloat
flows southward and the Reedy River meets the Slow-River.
You, please do not unfasten my brocade bindings,
with the quick rapids the boat will go as lightning.

Reedy waters meet slow waters,
joining together they are the same as one body,
I desire to recline in the boat with you
and be a person of Naniwa for a long time.

[The man speaks, in the style of a Japanese poem.]

You are like plum blossoms on water,
blossoms floating on water are quick to pass by.
I am like a willow tree beside the river.
My shadow sinks into the water and cannot follow you.

This poem was first published in 1777.

SPRING WIND ON THE RIVERBANK OF KEMA
(*Shunpu Batei Kyoku*)

One day I was going to visit an old man in my homeland. I crossed the sluggish river and was going along the riverbank of Kema when I happened to catch up with a woman on her way home for a visit. Passing each other from time to time for some distance, we began conversing. She appeared charming and her figure was attractive. As a result I made a song of eighteen parts, which I offer in her voice, as an expression of her own feelings.

(I)
Back to a land of fields!
On my visit from Naniwa,
the Nagara River.

(II)
Spring wind—
the riverbank goes on and on
and home is far.

(III)
Leaving the riverbank to pick fragrant grasses,
thorny bushes with vines obstruct my way.
With what jealousy the entwined thorny bushes
tear at the hem of my robe and scratch at my thighs.

(IV)

On entering a stream with scattered rocks,
stepping on rocks, I pick scented cresses.
I am thankful to the rocks in the water
for keeping my robe edge from getting wet.

(V)

One hut, where tea is sold—
the willow tree beside it
became old!

(VI)

The tea shop's old woman, seeing me, politely says
she is glad for my safety and admires my spring robe.

(VII)

Two customers are inside the shop
who understand the southern riverside language.
Leaving three strings of coins behind,
they let me have their bench when they go.

(VIII)

Old houses, two or three—
a cat calls for his mate,
but no mate comes.

(IX)

From outside a fence, a hen calls her fledglings.
Outside the fence, grass covers the land.
Fledglings are eager to flutter over the fence.
The fence is high and three or four fall back.

(X)

Grassy spring paths, three of them coming together—
one is a quicker way
and it invites me.

(XI)

Dandelions blooming—three, three, five, five.
Five, five—yellow. Three, three—white.
Remembering in a former year I left by this path.

(XII)

Cherishing memories, I pick a dandelion,
white milk spreading from the short stem.

(XIII)

Long long ago, my mother's tender care,
eagerly I think of it.
Held close within my mother's clothing
there was a different kind of spring.

(XIV)
In the spring,
since growing up
I lived in Naniwa.

Plum blossoms are white
by a Naniwa bridge,
a wealthy man's house.
I became used to springtime feelings
as they are in Naniwa.

(XV)
Leaving home,
neglecting brother
for three springtimes.

Forgetting its main trunk
I took a twig
of a plum tree for grafting.

(XVI)
In the homeland spring has deepened.
I go on and on, go on and on.

Willow trees on the long river banks.
The road goes downward gradually.

(XVII)
Raising my head I see the first glimpse,
my home and garden in the dusk.

Leaning against the door an old person with white hair
holds onto my brother while waiting for me
spring after spring.

(XVIII)
Do you not know old Taigi's haiku?
"Back to the land of fields
for a visit, sleeping
beside a lone priest."

This long poem by Buson was first published in 1777. It combines Japanese haiku and Chinese quatrains and some stanzas contain elements of both. Not all scholars are in agreement on the meaning and form of each section and the translation may be considered experimental.

SELECTIONS
FROM THE PROSE OF BUSON

From the Preface to
The Collected Haiku of Shundei

[Shundei Kushu jo]
(Written in 1777)

Kuroyanagi Korekoma edited his late father's manuscript and asked me to do its preface. So I write. I once met Kuroyanagi Shoha [Shundei] at his villa in the west suburbs of Kyoto. At that time he questioned me about *haikai*. I answered that the essence of *haikai* is to use ordinary words and yet to become separate from the ordinary. Be separate from the ordinary and still use the ordinary.

How to become separate from the ordinary is most difficult. A well-known Zen priest said, "You should try to listen to the sound of one hand clapping." This is the Zen of *haikai* and the way of being separated from the ordinary.

Shoha understood, and again questioned. "What you, old master, told me about how to become separate from the ordinary is profound, but it is still something we have to attain by our own efforts, isn't it? Is there any easy way to a shorter road to detachment from the ordinary?"

I answered, "Yes. You should read Chinese poetry. You have been good at Chinese poetry for a long time. There is no other way than that."

Shoha dared to ask, "Chinese poetry and *haikai* are different, and yet you say we should abandon *haikai* and read Chinese poetry. Isn't it a roundabout way?"

I answered, "Painters [Buson was referring to painters of land-scapes in the Southern Sung style] have a theory of detaching the ordinary, which says, 'While painting there is no other way to exclude the ordinary than to read many books, then the atmosphere from the books becomes superior and the atmosphere of ordinary cities becomes inferior. Those who want to learn should follow this way.' Even painters throw away their brushes and read books in order to exclude the ordinary. So Chinese poetry and *haikai*, why should they be apart."

Shoha understood at once.

One day he questioned me again. "Since old times there have been many different gateways to *haikai* and each is different. Which gateway shall I enter to reach that pavilion's innermost room?"

I answered, "There are no gateways to *haikai*. There is only the haikai gateway itself. Here I will quote a theory of fine art. 'Great artists do not set up a gateway [school]. A gateway exists naturally.' It is the same with *haikai*. Take all the streams into your water bag and keep them and choose for yourself what is good and use it for your purposes. Think for yourself about what you have inside yourself. There is no other way. But still, if you don't choose appropriate friends to communicate with, it is difficult to reach that world."

Shoha asked, "Who are the friends?"

I answered, "Call on Kikaku, visit Ransetsu, recite with Sodo, accompany Onitsura [Basho's associates, all dead at this time.] Day after day you should meet these four old poets and get away from the distracting atmosphere of the cities. Wander around the forests and drink and talk in the mountains. It is best if you acquire haiku naturally. Thus should you spend every day and some day you will meet the four poets again. Your appreciation of nature will be unchanged. Then you will close your eyes and seek for words. When you get haiku, you will open your eyes. Suddenly the four poets will have disappeared. No way of knowing where they became supernatural. You stand there alone in an ecstasy. At that time, flower fragrance comes with the wind and moonlight hovers on the water. This is the world of *haikai*."

Shoha smiled.

A Record of the Rebuilding of Basho's Grass Hut, in Eastern Kyoto
(Rakuto Basho-an Saiko-ki)

At the southwestern foot of Mt. Hiei, in Ichijo-ji Village, there is a Zen temple named Konpokuji. Local people customarily call it the Basho Hut Temple. At the beginning of the staircase, where we climb up the jade hillside for twenty steps, there is a mound of soil. This is known as the site of Basho's hut. It is, of course, a quiet and serene place with green mosses, which hide the human footsteps of a hundred years. The dark bamboo forest looks as though in it steam still lingers from his tea kettle.

Water goes and clouds stay; trees are old; birds sleep. Such things make us long for the old days. It is away from the center of the capital city, of striving for fame and riches, and yet, the surroundings do not exclude the city dust completely. Chickens and dogs call from beyond the bamboo fence, and the trail for wood cutters and ox herders passes by the gate. A small house that sells tofu is near, and a shop for buying sake is not far off either. It is convenient for poets and guests to come here and indulge in quietness for half a day, as it is so easy to get supplies to keep from becoming hungry.

When and how did people start to call it the Basho Hut? Every time I inquire of weed-cutting boys and wheat-thrashing women about the Basho Hut, they all point toward here. It certainly must be an old name. And yet, people do not know why it is called thus.

I happened to overhear that in old times a great priest named Tesshu used to live in this temple and that he made a room apart for himself and enjoyed a humble life there; doing laundry and cooking with his own hands, and excusing himself from visitors, he hid himself away inside. Whenever he read haiku by the old Basho, he shed tears and thought, "How precious. I also can attain the state of ignoring society and acquiring Zen." He often used to say this.

About this time, the venerable Basho traveled east and west of Yamashiro Providence [Kyoto area], reciting poems, washing the dust from his eyes with the waters of Kiyotaki [gorge], feeling the passing of time with the clouds of Arashiyama. Also he visited the wooden statue of the poet Jozan [Shisendo Temple] and wrote a poem about the fresh feeling of the statue's summer robe in the balmy air. Near the old grave of Chosho, he felt sympathy for a lone priest out begging on a cold night. Too, he wrote the poem about himself that begins, "Who is it wearing a straw mat?" as well as the one, "Yesterday was your crane stolen—," using an artistic legend from the Kozan Mountains in China. He traveled with walking stick around the foot of Mt. Hiei, shaking the morning mists from his hempen sleeves; he saw the view of Lake Biwa with gazing eyes like those of the poet Tu Fu. Eventually, he came to Karasaki, and with the poem about a blurred view of far off pine trees, he reached the supreme stage of his poetry.

Perhaps he thought this place was convenient for his purposes of wandering around Kyoto, occasionally resting here on a rock. But when, with his last poem, "My dream of withered fields," he passed away, that great priest [Tesshu] grieved and named the grass room "Basho's Hut" so that Basho's art would be treasured for long and would not be forgotten. I hear there were similar cases in the foreign country [China], such as naming a hut for the pleasure of getting rainfall after dry days. As far as we know, no haiku that he made here exists. Also, there are no manuscripts of his brush writing of poems. I don't think we can prove anything definitely about this hut.

The master priest Reverend Shoso says, "You know, 'Let me feel lonely,/ your singing voice,/ kanko-bird,' was a poem made when Basho was staying in this temple. It was what the late old priest who was learned in the way of letters told me. So why wouldn't brush writing with ink, which can stand dew and frost, last in spite of the running waters of the years? But Zen priests with rough minds seek for truth not by words, and they throw away even the sutras of Buddha. So they may feel, why should we keep such a little thing for long. Such non-artistic, rough people might have thrown it into the trash box, or neglected it, so that it became worm eaten and decayed. It is a regretful matter," he told me sadly.

Well, after all, these poems cannot be traced. In such a beautiful place, Basho's precious name is still kept. If we abandon that, it is a wrong, and in time, I talked to friends with the same opinion; thus, for the purpose of cherishing the high art of this venerable poet, we rebuilt the grass hut and decided to meet here in this temple without fail in the beginning of the fourth month, for the *hototogisu*, and in the ninth month, for the crying deer.

The head man in charge of the rebuilding is Doryu. I heard that Doryu's great-grandfather, Tan-an Sensei, was the teacher by whom Basho was taught to read Chinese characters. Thinking of this, the fact that Doryu is engaged with this event may be a karma matter from his previous life.

An-ei 5 (1776), the fifth month,
two days before the full moon.
Sincerely written by
Yahantei-Buson, Heian [Kyoto].

Visiting Uji
[Uji-ko]

To the south of Mt. Uji, deep in the mountains, I went to a village called Tahara for autumn mushroom hunting. Young people were greedily hurrying ahead to find their quarry while I, being left far behind, quietly looked from place to place. I found five mushrooms as big as small grass hats. How splendid! I wondered why Chief Councillor of State, Lord Uji Takakuni, wrote only about the strangeness of hiratake mushrooms and forgot about the splendor of matsutake mushrooms.

> You should see
> the five mushrooms with dew-drops
> that were not picked!

On the very top of the mountain, people's houses were seen in a place called Ko-no-o village. I was told they manage to live in this world from *ayu* fish which they catch in a basket. Reed thatched roofs look as though towering up to the clouds. A fragile bridge hangs over the water. Even in such a remote place people are living. It gave shivers to this traveler's being.

> The *ayu* have gone downstream
> and higher and higher
> the mountain ridges!

At the place called Komekashi is the most rapid torrent in the Uji River. Water and rocks struggle with each other, and splashing and leaping waves make a spray like flying snow, similar to hovering clouds. The sound roaring in the gorge overpowers human voices.

> "A silver jar gets broken and water rushes out.
> Horse soldiers in metal armor rattle swords.
> Four strings make a single cry like a tearing
>   of silk."

Thus the Chinese poet Po Chu-i described the enchanting music of the *biwa*. Thinking about his marvelous poem, I wrote:

> A tearing of silk—
> streaming out from a *biwa*
> the voice of autumn.

This was written by Buson in 1783, about four months before his death.
A biwa is a Japanese short-necked fretted lute.

FROM *New Flower Picking*
(Shin Hanatsumi)
(Written in 1777)
[Simple tales, sometimes with the supernatural or humor]

I.

A man named Jou in Yuki set up a mansion and had an old caretaker stay there. Even though it was in town, trees and bushes grew there thickly and it was a convenient place for getting away from city crowds. Once, I stayed in that place for a while. While the old man, who took care of the place and had nothing to do except clean the house floors with a wet cloth, was fingering his Buddhist rosary under a single lantern during a leisurely autumn evening, I was in a back room making haiku and struggling to do a Chinese poem. By and by, I became tired and pulled a quilt over myself and dozed off. Then there was a pounding and pounding at the rain shutter by the corridor. About twenty or thirty repeated knocks. I felt very puzzled and my heart pounded, but I got up from the bed and opened the door stealthily and tried to see what it was, but there was nothing.

Again I went to bed and tried to sleep; then, just as before, there was pounding and pounding. Again I got up, but could not see even a shadow of anything.

Because it was so frightening, I told the old man and asked him what to do about it. He exclaimed, "So he came again! It is the badger! When he comes again and pounds you should open the door quickly and chase him. I will go around to the back door and hide myself behind the hedge and wait." He took a bamboo pole and went to wait for the return of the badger. I pretended to be taking a badger nap and waited too.

Again there came a pounding and pounding. "There!" I opened the door while the old man dashed out saying, "Here he is!" But we didn't see anything. The old man became annoyed and looked from one corner to another of the garden. We didn't find even a shadow. Thus we spent every night for five nights, and I became exhausted and decided I couldn't stay there any longer.

Then Jou's head servant came from the city house and said, "That creature shouldn't come tonight. At daybreak today in Yabushita [Under-the-woods], the villagers killed an old badger. I suppose it was he who bothered you so much recently. Tonight I hope you will sleep peacefully."

As expected, there was no pounding after that night. Although I had been annoyed with the creature, I felt compassion for the thing that visited me when I was all alone at night during my stay. I felt it might have been a part of my karma. So I hired a priest named Zenkubo and gave him a donation for a night service to bring peace to the spirit of the badger.

> Autumn dusk—
> turned into a Buddha image
> a badger!

People say a badger pounds on a door with his tail, but it is not true. It is the sound made by bumping his back against a door.

II.

Once I stayed at a temple called Kenshoji, in Miyazu, Tango, for a little more than three years. From the beginning of one autumn, I suffered from a fever for about fifty days. Inside the temple, at the back, was a very spacious room with floor matting, and the doors were always closed tight, with not even space for air to get through. I was in bed sick next to that room, and the sliding doors between that back room and my room were closed tightly.

Once, about two o'clock in the morning, my fever being a little lower, I decided to go alone to the toilet and got up onto my unsure feet. Leading to the toilet at the northwest corner of the building, there was a long hallway going beside that spacious room. With the lantern out, it was very dark. I opened the sliding door, and then, as I made the first step with my right foot, I stepped on something furry and round. I was so surprised that I drew back my foot and tried to see what it was, but there was no sound at all.

Though startled and frightened, I tried to calm myself. Stepping again, this time with my left foot, I kicked out powerfully where I thought the thing was. But nothing at all touched me. I was even more mystified, and with all my body hair standing upright, shuddering and shuddering, I went into the priest's room and woke him and his attendants from their sound sleep and told them all about it. Then everybody got up, and with many lighted lamps, we went to that back room and looked. But all the fusuma and shoji were closed with no open spaces. Not even the shadow of something strange was found.

Everybody said to me, "You have a fever and say things that are crazy nonsense." They all became angry and went to bed again. Thinking I shouldn't have told them of such things and feeling embarrassed, I went back to bed, too. When I was almost asleep, I felt a heaviness, as though a big rock were on my chest, and I moaned and moaned. As my fussing was heard, the head priest, Reverend Chikukei, came in, saying, "Wake up! What is the matter?" He helped me to sit up, and when I recovered myself, I told him about what had disturbed me.

"I know what it was. That naughty badger did it!" He opened a door and looked outside. The day was already breaking whitely, and we could plainly see that from the open corridor to the wooden veranda there were small footprints like scattered petals of plum blossoms. Then the rest of the people of the temple realized what had been the matter and were very surprised, although they had ridiculed me for nonsense before.

When I had moaned, the Reverend Chikukei had hurried to me in the darkness with his sash untied and kimono open in front, and now, his round testicles were seen like rice bags. White hairs were growing over them so that his important part was hidden. Since his youth he had had the itch there and had always been pulling and scratching at himself. He looked like that famous Shukaku priest did when he dozed from reading Buddhist sutras. With such thoughts, I felt embarrassed, but then the Reverend Chikukei laughed and recited:

> "Autumn again [hanging down!]
> Camphor wood of eight mats size [badger's balls],
> the Golden Pavilion Temple [itching balls]."

III.

At Shimodate, in the province of Hitachi [Ibaraki], there lived a man named Nakamura Hyozaemon. He was at that time a disciple of the late Hayano Hajin [a haiku poet who was a teacher of Buson] and was fond of *haikai*. He took as his poet-name Huko, Bamboo-in-the-wind. He was the richest man in his neighborhood and his luxurious house was two blocks square. For both front and back gardens, he collected unusual looking rocks and trees; he had made a pond where he freed birds; and his miniature mountain was described as a real beauty of nature. Occasionally, the provincial governor paid visits there. Nakamura Hyozaemon was really an unrivaled man of wealth.

His wife, who was a daughter of a rich merchant named Fuji, was called Omitsu. She had had training in *waka* poetry and stringed instruments and was of a gracious and tender nature.

Although they were rich, in time, the family lost its power and was left to itself, with few people coming to visit. At the time of the beginning of this family decline, there were several strange incidents. Among them was a fearful event that makes the body hair stand upright. One year in December, in preparation for the new year, the family made more *omochi* rice-cakes than in usual years and stored them in a number of large wooden tubs. But each night some of the cakes disappeared, and there was much concern as to who could have stolen them. They put a heavy wooden board like a door over each tub, and on top of each of these, they put a large rock. The next morning when, with unsure feelings, they uncovered the tubs to look, the cakes were half gone, although the coverings were found still in the same positions as on the night before. At that time the husband, Huko, was engaged in business matters and was staying in Edo. Because of this, his wife, Omitsu, was dutifully keeping house and was a kind supervisor to the servants. Everyone felt sorry for her and often there were tears of sympathy.

One night, she was making the new year's clothes out of a beautiful silk. As it was growing late, she gave permission for all the servants to go to bed. She went alone into one of the rooms, closing all the doors so no openings were left, and there, with a bright lamp, she quietly sewed the clothing. Only the dripping of the water-clock made a sound. When it was about two o'clock in the morning, five or six very old, withered foxes with dragging tails passed by in front of her knees. Of course, every door and sliding panel was tightly closed; there was no open chink anywhere. How could they have crept in? Startled, she intently watched them move by as though crossing a wide field with nothing in their way, and soon, they disappeared, just fading away. Not feeling very frightened, Omitsu resumed sewing as before.

The next morning when someone called at the house and said comfortingly, "How are you? As your husband is slow to return, you must be feeling uneasy." Omitsu, looking even more beautiful than usual, calmly told all about the strange thing that she had seen the night before. The visitor commented, "Even hearing about it makes one's neck chilly. How peculiar! With such a strange thing happening, why didn't you wake up your servants instead of enduring it all by yourself? Unlike a woman, you were very strong minded!"

Her answer was, "Not at all. I didn't feel the least bit frightened." Usually, even when rain hit against a shutter or a gust of wind rustled the bushes, she felt frightened and pulled the bed quilt over her head. But on only that night she did not feel disturbed. It was really, really a strange thing.

IV.

There was an old poet, a disciple of Kaiga [a follower of Basho] named Hayami Shinga. One night when he stayed at Huko's house, his bed was in the front guest room. It was the eighteenth night of the ninth month. The moon was clear and dewdrops were cool; on the bushes of the front garden, crickets were singing. The autumn mood was so moving that he kept the wooden rain shutters open and went to bed with only the paper doors closed. About one o'clock, he happened to lift his head from the pillow and look around, The moon was still so bright that it looked like midday, and in a row on the veranda were sitting a number of foxes waving their round hairy tails, their shadows plainly showing on the paper sliding doors, and he felt utterly frightened. Feeling it impossible to endure more, Shinga rushed out into the kitchen, knocked at the door of a room where he thought his host was sleeping, and called out, "You there, you there! Please get up," as loudly as he could. The servants woke up and made a big fuss, saying "Thieves, it must be thieves!" With their noise, Shinga felt calm again and, looking with fully awakened eyes, realized he was knocking at the toilet door, asking loudly, "Sire, please get up and help me."

Later he talked of this, saying, "It was really very embarrassing."

V.

The governor of the castle of Shirakawa, Matsudaira Yamato-no-Kami, had a retainer named Akimoto Gohei. He was an expert at *kendo*. Having had a little trouble with his master, he quit his service and left the province. As he liked *haikai*, he changed his name to Suigetsu [moon-intoxicated] and wandered around the Gumma and Chiba area, becoming acquainted with wealthy families here and there, living like drifting water-weeds and windblown grasses, and not settling into one dwelling place. He was actually a man of elegant tastes. This elderly man, also, once stayed in the back room at Huko's house. While in bed, he sensed that about three old women were together beside the veranda; the sounds of their whispering were heard all night. He wondered what they were talking about and strained his ears to hear it, but he couldn't understand any of their words. As the night deepened, he felt somehow very sorry for them and couldn't go to sleep until daybreak.

Selections from Buson's Letters

From a letter written to Kafu and Otofusa, 1775
[In this particular year an extra month was added for calendar adjustment]

Nowadays, traveling *haikai* poets have a mean scheme that no other people have. The reason is that at every place they visit they want to grab money [for correcting haiku and being entertained]. There is nothing else on their minds. They will do anything to gain what they want. They just explain how good they are and how poor other poets are and hope to be believed. "Please give me money," they almost beg for it.

Anyway, this can be harmful, and people living in remote places cannot tell the differences among *haikai* persons and may be wrongly influenced and misled. You two already know well about such things and are not endangered, but please be careful always.

You said the sea by your place is rough and no fish can be caught. Whenever you have extra, please send me some. The little wild ducks you sent me last year were especially delicious, Otofusa, and I cannot forget them. If you get some please send one.

This letter became longer than expected. Your letter came after a long silence and comforted my old mind, and I felt my headache had been chased away. So, although in my sick bed, I have been writing a long letter. If I become well, I will write my opinion about our group poem and show it to you. For the present, please excuse me. The above is all.

Eleventh day of the Thirteenth month,
Buson to Kafu and Otofusa

Thank you for your frequent messages to my wife and daughter. My daughter is taking koto lessons and has made a lot of progress. Even in this cold weather she plays, and it is noisy to my ears, but I am glad she has safely become an adult.

This year, not many haiku have been done, but even so, I have five or ten. The haiku done since autumn, I probably sent in my last letter, if so, it would be a repetition, so I will not include them here.

FROM A LETTER, WRITTEN BY BUSON TO TOSHI,
A DISCIPLE, 1776.

The other day I received your detailed letter. On the occasion of the wedding reception [for Buson's daughter] at my house, there were thirty-four or -five guests. Among them was the best unrivaled koto performer of Kyoto; also, there were five or six *maiko* dancers [apprentice geishas]. It was a big banquet filled with beauties, and it lasted until cock-crow in the morning. After that, for four or five days, the host [Buson] was exhausted and passed the time as if he were mud.

Because of this, I could not write to you sooner. Please understand. When you came to Kyoto I was looking forward to your visit, but without making one, you went back to Naniwa. Although I assume you were busy, I regret it greatly. These days, I am steadfastly engaged in painting and scarcely any haiku are written. It is not a very poetic way of life.

First, I appreciated with real interest your writing about visiting Takao [western suburbs of Kyoto]. Please give my sincere regards to Shunsaku and Akinari [author of *Ugetsu Monogatari*]. I think your haiku about the night with frost on the road of Gose is one of the best of your recent works.

[signed] Shiko
[Purple Fox, one of
Buson's artist names]

FROM A LETTER WRITTEN IN THE SECOND MONTH, TWENTY-THIRD DAY, 1777

Kema is my home village. When I was a child, on lovely spring days, I always went to this [Yodo] river bank with friends and played there. There were boats going up and down on the water.

On the banks, people were coming and going, among them country girls who worked as housemaids in Naniwa and imitated the fashionable styles of that city. Their hair was done in the style of *maiko*, and they loved romantic tales and gossip. Although they were ashamed of the brothers they had left at home, their longings to return could not be denied, and they paid occasional visits to the villages of their parents.

A LETTER WRITTEN TO TWO OF BUSON'S DISCIPLES, MASANA AND SHUNSAKU, 1777

We haven't corresponded for quite a while. Indeed, the rainy season has made difficulties. I imagine you suffered too. I am glad both of you are all right now. My situation has not changed. As I haven't had a letter since then, I was wondering how you are. Because of your temple matter, I assume you have no leisure time. About Tairo's incident, I assume you have heard quite a lot. As you have imagined, his future is quite uncertain. I feel sorry about it.

How is your poetry? I haven't received any of your poems for a long time. Although I am forced to do paintings, I let days go by without often taking up my haiku brush, and because of this, my painting work cannot progress too well either. Poverty's ghost haunts me, but I feel fortunate.

The painting Shunsaku asked me to do has not been completed. Please forgive me for postponing it. Soon I will show you the work.

As for my daughter, the old man of her husband's family

is very mercenary and insincere. And many things went against my will, so I took her back from them. Of course, my daughter herself could not endure that family's ways and had been sick and weak. Well, you know, money is nothing if her life cannot last. I felt sorry for her and so took her back. As you have been kind, I inform you of this.

Please give my regards to your wife. My wife sends greetings, too. There have been no changes in my circumstances, but as I wonder about you, I am writing this letter. Further news about things here will be in my next letter.
I bow to you with my neck bent down.

[signed] Buson
Twenty-fourth day,
the fifth month

To Masana and Shunsaku

Rainfall in May!
Facing a big river,
houses, two of them.

Cool feeling!
Detached from a bell
the sound of the bell.

These are not in the fashionable style. Too much fashion is annoying.

> Moon after rainfall.
> Who is it at night
> with white limbs?

They are not very interesting, but I include them here. By the way, how is Mucho [Ueda Akinari] these days? I haven't heard from him for a long time. Please give him my kind regards.

FROM A LETTER WRITTEN TO DORYU, A FRIEND, 1780

Your opinion that I should renounce the house of beauty is quite sensible, I think. According to your advice, today I shall give up my longing for *koito* [geisha]. Because of my useless romantic feeling, I lost my dignity in my old age. I should forbid myself. . .

> twenty-fifth day,
> the fourth month
> Buson to Doryu

BUSON AND HIS WRITINGS

YUKI SAWA

When discussing Buson, most people compare him with Basho. It may be similar to the fact that when discussing Brahms, one cannot help comparing him with Beethoven. Indeed, Basho was the poet who brought *haikai* from an undeveloped stage to a mature and enriched art of poetry.

That Buson, born about seventy years after Basho, respected Basho's poetry all through his life is evident by his own words: "I shall seek only for the elegant simplicity and sensitivity of old master Basho and restore *haikai* back to what it was in the ancient days." (Preface to *Mukashi O Ima*, 1774.) In the same year, he also said, "If I neglect to recite old master Basho's poems for three days, I get thorny mouthed." (Preface to *Basho-o-Tsukeaishu*, 1774.)

Yet, a year before, he had written in a letter, "This old man's *haikai* do not intend to closely follow old master Basho's style. I just go by my own will and enjoy the different atmospheres of yesterday and today." (Buson's letter to a haiku poet, Kato Kyotai, at Nagoya.)

Reading his writings, it can be understood that, although Buson paid great respect to Basho's poetry, he was aware his own *haikai* were quite different. Buson and Basho do seem similar, yet they're far from being alike. Many have mentioned the differences between them. Some have said Buson is more modern, while Basho is more medieval. Dr. Teruoka Yasutaka termed Buson an intellectual epicurean and Basho a stoic. Others have described Buson as a poet of spring and summer and Basho as a poet of autumn and winter. Still others have said Buson is pictorial and Basho musical. The poet

Murano Shiro calls Buson a lyric colorist and Basho an artist of black and white. These words do not explain everything, but they help us realize several aspects of the two poets.

Buson did not consciously try to write haiku that were different from Basho's. He respected Basho and tried to get closer to his poetry, yet, he could not help but realize the difference between Basho and himself. This can be seen in Kito's writing about Buson's last days:

> Also, he once said to his night nurse, "Even being sick like this, my fondness for the way is beyond reason, and I try to make haiku. The heights of 'My dream hovers over withered fields' [Basho's last haiku] is impossible for me to reach. Therefore, the old poet Basho's greatness is supremely moving to me now."

Let us consider several haiku by Buson and Basho. In 1694, when fifty-year-old Basho, in his final illness, was in his bed at a house in Osaka, he wrote his last haiku:

> Being ill on a journey
> my dreams run wandering
> through withered fields.

Buson's last haiku, composed in his bed in his own house in Kyoto when dying at the age of sixty-seven in 1783, can be translated:

With white plum blossoms
these nights to the faint light of dawn
are turning.

These two poems show to a considerable extent the difference between the poets. Just before his death, Basho imagined in his mind desolate fields, while Buson thought of the faint dawn light fragrant with white plum blossoms. Buson's last haiku sounds the more peaceful.

Another comparison can be made between haiku concerned with early summer rainfall. Basho's is well known:

Early summer rain—
accumulating as it swiftly flows,
the Mogami River.

About a similar scene Buson wrote:

Early summer rain—
facing toward the big river,
houses, two of them.

Basho described the movement of a swelling river; Buson made a pictorial composition, placing two houses close to a large river. For another example, a haiku by Basho:

A flooded rice field,
now its planting is done I leave—
the willow tree.

The poem was based on a *waka*, or *tanka*, by the 12th century wandering priest-poet Saigyo, who, on a journey to the northern part of Japan, happened to rest under a willow tree and made a poem about it:

> Beside the road
> a flowing of clear water,
> in a willow's shade
> I thought for just a short while
> to linger and take a rest.

This *waka* of Saigyo was so admired that the place where he rested by the willow tree became legendary. Some hundreds of years later, in the seventeenth century, another traveling poet, Basho, visited what was reputed to be the same willow tree and wrote the previously quoted haiku. In Japan, many places that were admired in medieval *waka* poems became famous and were visited by later poets and gave a foundation to their poetic imaginations.

This particular willow tree was visited by Buson, about fifty years after Basho did, and he also wrote a haiku:

> The willow leaves fall
> and the clear water has gone,
> stones lie everywhere.

When we compare Buson's poem with Basho's, it can be said that Buson's is much more pictorial and appeals to the visual imagination. On a summer day, willow leaves fall, and beneath, the river has dried up and the stones are exposed. In Basho's haiku, the poet rests under the willow tree and watches the rice-planting girls at work. He forgets himself, and after a while realizes the rice is all planted and is surprised at the passing of time. This poem does not appeal to our sense of sight. Instead, in this poem the flow of time is expressed.

I do not intend to say that Buson is always more pictorial than Basho. When we consider Basho's:

> On a withered tree branch
> a crow perches—
> autumn dusk.

and Buson's:

> A mountain pheasant
> moves his feet on the branch—
> the long night!

we can say that Basho's poem is the more pictorial.

What is more noteworthy are the differences in their personalities. Basho was a man who could say, "I followed this single path because I had not other talent or ability" (in a travelogue *Oi no Kobumi* and in an essay *"Genjuan no Ki"*). Buson was excellent in both haiku and painting, and he also had many pleasures, such as drinking with friends and going to theaters with *maiko* girls. That he sometimes even played at being an actor when his wife and daughter were not at home is related in an essay by a painter who also lived in Edo times.

Buson's versatile temperament may be sensed in this haiku:

> On my coming back,
> how many pathways are there
> through the spring grasses?

The fact that Buson was more versatile than Basho can be better understood if considered against the background of the times.

The government of the Tokugawa shogunate began in the early seventeenth century. Basho lived in the latter half of that century. In those early days of the Edo period, intellectual young men who were not born into a samurai family or who couldn't inherit their father's positions because they weren't the first born-son could elevate themselves by studying either Confucian philosophy or medicine, or both. They might then be hired by the central government or one of the provincial governments.

Around the start of the eighteenth century, the social structure became more rigid and saturated. There were few opportunities for young people because the professions were being passed on from father to son. Those already in official work found it difficult to get positions that were better or more suited to their talents. Such limitations affected not only the intelligentsia but also the merchant class.

In the latter half of the seventeenth century, in the time

of Basho and Saikaku, there had been considerable freedom in commercial activities, as described in one of Saikaku's novels:

> Indeed, the rice trading market in Kitahama, since it is the biggest port in Japan, deals by direct negotiations in fifty thousand silver Kan worth of rice every hour or two. That amount of rice packed in straw bags is piled up like mountains and stored in warehouses. As the price of rice is affected by the weather, people watch evening storms and morning rainfalls, consider the sunlight and the passing of the clouds, and think things over during the night. Some go for selling, others go for buying. They fight over a difference of one or two percent and crowd together like a mountain.

As time passed, the power of the Tokugawa government, whose foundations were based on the rice collected as taxation from farmers, gradually was surpassed by the big merchants in Osaka who controlled the economy. To offset this, the government confiscated the assets of a wealthy and powerful Osaka merchant named Yodoya and then made a law by which a samurai's debts to merchants could be cancelled. Consequently, the merchant class became conservative in their business, and with their surplus energy, many of these affluent businessmen became interested in learning and the arts. What these intellectuals studied was Chinese poetry and prose, ancient Japanese literature, and natural history, especially botany. Many took up brushes to paint in the Chinese literati style. They did not renounce their daily occupations, but did these new activities on the side.

It should be mentioned, too, that at this time Japan was still prohibiting almost all contact with foreigners. When Buson lived, such was the atmosphere in the arts. Buson was a professional painter, and at the same time, he was productive in *haikai*. To refine his haiku, he read Chinese poetry. That his interest in Chinese poetry was of considerable importance to him is shown clearly in his preface to the *Collected Haiku of Shundei*. When Buson's disciple, Shoha, questioned him about *haikai*, Buson answered, "The essence of *haikai* is to use ordinary words and yet to become separate from the ordinary." When Shoha asked further about a shorter road to detachment from the ordinary, Buson answered, "You should read Chinese poetry."

Buson stressed the importance of reading Chinese classic poetry because he wanted to overcome the vulgar sort of *haikai* being followed by such haiku teachers as Bakurin and Shiko. After Basho's death, *haikai* poets forgot Basho's high standards and wrote haiku in a superficially refined or a joking way. Basho had also read Chinese poetry, especially that of the eighth century poet Tu Fu, but the way in which Buson appreciated Chinese poetry was a little different from his. Buson's emphasized reading many books so that the atmosphere in the books becomes more important than the atmosphere of ordinary places. Basho, on the other hand, is reputed to have stressed the importance of the experience of life itself, saying, "Those who have no traveling experience along the Tokaido [the old inter-city highway] are quite unlikely to become good at poetry."

Buson's familiarity with Chinese poetry shows in his haiku, sometimes in direct ways and sometimes in indirect ways.

> *Ascending the Eastern Slope*
> Flowering thorn—
> the path by my home village
> is like this!

In the preface to this haiku he mentions "the eastern slope" (*toko*), a term written with a special Chinese character that had been used by the old Chinese poets T'ao Yuan-ming and Wang Wei. When he used this term, he was obviously thinking of these poets and identifying with them.

In another haiku he wrote:

> Darkness on the blossoms—
> back to Kyoto where I live
> now I will return.

In this poem, the term "now I will return" (*kaen'nan*) is taken from the first line of a well-known piece by T'ao Yuan-ming.

Even on his death bed he was thinking about Wang Wei.

Winter *uguisu*—
long ago in Wang Wei's
garden hedge too!

Chinese flavors appear not only in Buson's haiku but also in two of his three longer poems, "Slow-River Song" and "Spring Wind on the River Bank of Kema." For many centuries, Japanese poets had expressed their feelings mainly in the short forms of *tanka* and haiku, except for *choka* (extended poems) in the eighth century collection of the *Manyoshu,* and *renga,* linked verse done by several poets together in the eleventh century and after. There was also another kind of poetry. Intellectual men, aristocrats and priests had, since the eighth century, used the Chinese language when writing poetry. This was still being practiced at the end of the nineteenth century. Especially around Buson's time, poets read Chinese poetry eagerly and wrote in Chinese forms. Buson wrote alternately haiku and Chinese style passages in his two longer poems.

In the poem "Spring Wind on the Riverbank of Kema" there is a poet's longing for his home. Buson wrote in a letter about this poem:

> As for "Spring Wind on the Riverbank of Kema," Kema is my home village. When I was a child, on lovely spring days I always went to this river bank with friends and played there.... This poem is about a journey by a girl from Naniwa

going to her parent's village home. And the landscape is like the one in a *kyogen* theater. The theater owner is this fellow, Yahantei. You may laugh about it. In fact, this poem is done because of the yearning of this foolish old man for the past.

A writer in the later Edo period wrote, "Buson wasted all his ancestor's assets and placed himself in a carefree life away from the teachings of the gods, the Buddha, the Sacred, and the Wise and was a vagabond who sold his fame and flattered the common people." His home villagers may have felt the same way about him, which might have made him feel awkward about visiting Kema.

Far more mature than this poem is the piece "Mourning for the Old Poet Hokuju." Hokuju was Buson's friend when he was in his twenties, and he died at the age of seventy-four, when Buson was twenty-nine. Whether this piece was written right after Hokuju's death or much later is not known. It was published in 1793, ten years after Buson's death, when Hokuju's son edited a book to commemorate the fiftieth anniversary of his father's funeral. The editor said this piece had been recently found in a family storehouse. Some of the poets who were Buson's contemporaries tried this kind of poetry, which is freer in form than haiku or Chinese poetry, but Buson's piece is far superior to any of theirs.

Although he was able to use this freer expression in poetry, Buson wrote only this one piece in this style and did not try again. It is regretful. About a hundred years later, in 1882, a group of professors in Tokyo published *Shintaishi-sho*, a collection of poems translated from the West. The book also included their own poems written under the direct influence of poets such as Gray, Longfellow, and Tennyson. This was the beginning of a freer style of Japanese poetry, but it cannot be considered mature poetry. However, long before this, Buson had written a much superior poem, but the Japanese had forgotten about it. Even poet and acclaimed critic Masaoka Shiki (1869–1902), who evaluated Buson highly as a poet, did not know of the existence of this piece as it was not rediscovered during his time. In this poem, vocabulary and lines do not follow a Chinese style at all, although the way Buson carried through his ideas below the surface may have been borrowed from Chinese poetry. On the other hand, in his two other longer poems, a number of lines were written in Chinese characters alone.

Why was it that Buson did not write more works like this? Was it only when he lost his dear friend that he felt his emotions could not be expressed within the usual form of the haiku?

In his later years Buson said, "In the way of *haikai* you should not always adhere to your master's method.... Those who do not understand this way say it is an error to go against the master's way."

Buson seems to have been a very happy man. His accomplishments in painting and haiku certainly gave him much satisfaction. His letters and the comments of his disciples show him as a warm person with a number of close friends with whom he could communicate freely. Although in his letters he often complained that he was short of money, as he undoubtedly was, either from his own means or as a guest of others, he was able to be a theater fan, attend drinking parties, and be in the company of *maiko* girls. Among all his writings, one of the most outstanding statements is used as the epigraph to this book: "What you want to acquire, you should dare to acquire.... It is quite unusual to have a second chance to materialize your desire."

Although he lived in feudal times when life was quite restricted, he had a very positive attitude toward life. Perhaps those days allowed more individual freedom than we realize. Both in his poetry and in his painting, by idealizing a past tradition, he was more or less able to bypass the restrictive influences of his environment and emerge as a freely creative man.

Haiku often contain hidden references to previous literature, places, sentiments, and other knowledge commonly shared by literate and literary people. These are evoked by the use of particular words or phrases, and the poems are enriched far beyond their actual words. One typical example of this in Buson has been pointed out by critic Yamamoto Kenkichi and Prof. Ogata Tsutomu in the following haiku:

> White blooming plum tree—
> since whose time has it been there
> just outside the hedge?

"Outside the hedge" often suggests a man standing outside the hedge of the house of his beloved. Also, "whose time" is supposed to refer to the old *waka* phrase "whose sleeve with the fragrance of plum blossoms," which suggests a romantic occasion.

Although the words "haikai" and "haiku" can be used with the same meaning, "haikai" is the word used in Edo times while "haiku" is a newer word coined by Masaoka Shiki in the late nineteenth century. "Haiku" does not include *renga*, linked verse.

Renga is usually done by more than one person. The first poem or section is in 5-7-5 syllables. Another poet links it with another verse of 7-7 syllables. The third verse is in 5-7-5 syllables again. This usually continues for at least thirty-six sections. The essence of this form is in how adequately each section is linked to the previous one, as well as the flavor of each verse itself. There are a number of rules in this style of poem to keep it interesting.

Around the time of Basho, the *renga* form was practiced very frequently, and many individuals made an independent poem out of the first section, which was called *hokku*. But in later years, as in Buson's time, writing *hokku* was more popular. *Hokku* is what is today called haiku. Buson's linked verse done with friends is not included in this book, since Buson's essence is more characteristically seen in his haiku.

That Buson continues to be of importance and value even to contemporary Japanese poets is affirmed by Murano Shiro, one of the major poets of the twentieth century, who spoke of Buson with warm intimacy in one of his essays:

Reading Buson's haiku:

> A peony fallen—
> on top of one another,
> two petals, three petals.

I remember being startled by its sharp, clear sense of the thing itself. There was amazement, and I wondered from where Buson's sense of this came—a sense that believes poetry can be created out of such description.... He expressed life-consciousness with clear lyric imagery. That objectiveness was indeed Buson's true merit.

Yuki Sawa
Kyoto, 1976

A Brief Biography

In addition to being among the two or three most honored haiku poets of Japan, Yosa Buson (1717–1783) was one of the best artists of the literati or "Southern painting" style (*nanga*). He lived during the middle part of the Edo period, which extended from 1603 to 1867, an era when Japan was ruled by the government of the Tokugawa family, which had established itself after long feudal warfare. In the beginning of this period, literature did not flourish, but by around 1680, the activities of the common citizens and their commercial successes made it possible to produce powerful writers, such as Saikaku in fiction and Chikamatsu in drama. Theater and all the popular arts became strong and specialized. At this time, the poet Matsuo Basho was writing haiku which by now have become familiar to readers in all countries.

The short poems of 5-7-5 syllables, known as haiku, had been brought to a high standard of art by Basho; he had raised haiku from its previous stage, where it was usually based on a play on words and a simple or vulgar humor, to a totally new level. There were several good haiku poets before him, such as Onitsura and Soin, but it was he who really established the characteristics that are known today.

After his death, most of Basho's disciples and many other poets who were writing haiku in various parts of Japan forgot the true simplicity and purity of haiku and went into an over refined sophistication or popular joke-making. It was about seventy years after Basho's death that Buson and his contemporaries attempted to return to Old Basho's spirit.

Buson is believed to have been born in 1716 at Kema, a suburb of Osaka, about thirty miles southwest of the old capital of Kyoto. That would be about twenty-two years after Basho's death. Perhaps because his life with his family had been unusual, Buson himself never gave a clear explanation about his birth. Some guess that he was the child of a well-to-do farmer and one of his household maids. Apparently he lost both of his parents while young, and when he was about twenty, he left home for Edo, a poor young man determined to study painting and haiku.

At about the age of twenty-one, he became a disciple of the famous and eccentric haiku poet Hayano Hajin, who had been a disciple of Basho's disciples Kikaku and Ransetsu. Buson wrote of him and his teaching in the preface of MUKASHI O IMA (1774).

> The late master Soa [Hajin] had studied under the Snow Hermit [Ransetsu] and stood like one of the three legs of a tripod along with Hyakuri and Kinpu. They all expressed a new spirit and were admired as *haikai* poets. People of the time were stirred and influenced by the styles of these three. Each became a leader of poetic fashion, but the common people were not expected to be like them. My master once lived in Kokucho in Edo, near the high bell tower, in a humble dwelling, contented with a leisurely life in the town. One frosty night,

being startled from sleep by the bell and even though in the dazed condition of an old man's sudden awaking, he talked with me about *haikai*. When I spoke of the unreasonable things of the world, he pretended not to be listening to me and looked absent-minded. He was, indeed, a really superior old man. One night while he was sitting formally, he told me, "In the way of *haikai* you should not always adhere to the master's method. In every case you should be different, and in an instant, you should continue on without regard to whether you are being traditional or innovative." With this striking statement I understood and came to know the freedom within *haikai*. Thus, what I demonstrate to my disciples is not to imitate Soa's casual way but to long for the *sabi* [elegant simplicity] and *shiori* [sensitivity] of Basho, with the intention of getting back to the original viewpoint. This means to go against the external and to respond to the internal. It is the Zen of *haikai* and the heart-to heart way.

Buson was acquainted with several haiku poets in the Chiba area also, and after Hajin's death in 1742, he made journeys into the nearby countryside and to the northern area of "Oku" where Basho had traveled and which he had made the subject of his most famous writing. From what still remains of his earliest paintings, we also know that during his youth Basho worked in various styles and acquired a knowledge of Chinese art as well as poetry; this was to continue to have a strong influence on him. He spent his youth painting and making haiku, thus forming the foundation of his future work.

In the early winter of 1751, when he was thirty-five, he moved to Kyoto, perhaps because he was eager to study art there or perhaps to be near his birthplace. Though he lived mostly in Kyoto, he spent three years, beginning in 1754, at Miyazu, a seacoast town north of Kyoto. Eventually, he traveled to the island of Shikoku to paint screens at a temple. Wherever he was, he continued to work to master the skill of painting. His work as a haiku poet was a rather secondary matter to him for some years. He first acquired fame as a painter, but only after having experimented with various Japanese and Chinese styles and while enduring the hardships and self-discipline of slowly developing his own mature style.

Since medieval times, it had been traditional in Japan for many artists and writers to live as social exiles, such as itinerant priests or other homeless wanderers. Basho had lived this way and remained somewhat of a wanderer who frequently traveled in priest's robes and sought a Buddhist kind of lessening of the ego. When he was young, Buson, too, was an unordained Buddhist priest of the Jodo (Pure Land) sect. In those days, intellectuals valued their freedom and often tried to create a world of poetry and painting where the mind could exist more freely, thus avoiding feeling limited by the restrictive social network. A similar way of life had long been known in China, where neo-Buddhism blended with Taoism, and was much written of by Chinese poets and painters as well as those of Japan.

By the time he was about forty-five, Buson felt sufficiently established as an artist to undertake marriage and support a family in a humble style. He married a woman named Tomo, but the exact date is uncertain, and little is known about her.

In 1770, when he was fifty-four, Buson, urged by his haiku friends and followers, took the poet-name "Yahantei," after the late poet Hayano Hajin. Now he became officially a leader of haiku poets in Kyoto. However, he seemed to feel that there was much vulgarity in the contemporary haiku world and continued to devote much of his energy to the painting of many of his finest works in the form of hand scrolls, hanging scrolls, albums, and six-fold screens. In 1771, he painted a famous set of ten screens with Ike no Taiga, the major literati artist of the time, who painted ten additional screens. He worked in various styles and continued to develop, his very best work in the *nanga* style not being done until after he was sixty-two; eventually, the quality of his painting was unsurpassed.

Sono Yuki Kage [Light from the Snow], a book of haiku by Buson and his friends, was published in 1772. The next year, *Kono Hotori* [Around Here] and *Ake Garasu* [A Crow at Dawn] were published. The latter was a large collection including poets outside Buson's group, such as Ryota in Edo, Kyotai in Nagoya, Bakusui in Kaga, and Chora in Ise. The preface was written by Kito. Later, Chora and Kyotai came to Kyoto to visit Buson and his friends and to compose linked verse together.

Buson's health became poor in the third month of 1775, when he was about fifty-nine. The following year, his only daughter, Kuno, married a merchant in Kyoto, and this unhappy marriage gave him much anxiety. *Zoku-Ake Garasu* [Another Crow at Dawn], including more of his haiku, was published at this time.

Some of his letters give us glimpses of his daily concerns. A letter to his friend and disciple Kito, written on the eleventh day of the eight month, 1776, contains an evaluation of his own work that shows us he had come to realize his value as a painter. The letter was accompanied by seventeen paintings that were to be sold.

> None of these pieces are ordinary. As for haiku style brush paintings, there is nobody who can match me. Please do not sell them cheaply. This is a matter that I would not tell anyone else, only to you I confide it.

In another letter, written to his friend Nobutoshi on the thirteenth day, twelfth month, 1776, he reveals something of his simple life and warm heartedness:

> This month, this silly old man arranged a marriage for his daughter and was quite busy. No haiku were done, and days were spent without doing anything. But it seemed a fortunate future for my daughter and a good place to send her, so that my old mind is relaxed. Just after the

New Year, I will be free, and the wish to visit
Yoshino with a walking stick is strongly in my
mind. But also I want to drop in at Naniwa. I
would like to see you in a leisurely way, and I am
looking forward to it.

His next book, *Yahan-Raku*, was in celebration of the new
year and included his longer poems "Spring Wind at the
Riverbank of Kema" and "Slow-River Song." In the fourth
month of 1777, he decided to keep a notebook, *Shin
Hanatsumi* [New Flower Picking], in which he would write
ten haiku a day for one hundred days as a discipline, perhaps
in memory of his mother. But he was unable to continue it
for more than seventeen days because of illness. Instead, he
filled the rest of the notebook with essays of his old memo-
ries. In the fifth month, his daughter divorced her husband
and returned to her father's home.

In 1782, he made a trip to the Yoshino mountains south-
west of Nara to view the cherry blossoms. He continued his
painting and haiku activities. In the autumn of the next year,
he was invited by one of his disciples to visit Uji, south of
Kyoto, to collect mushrooms, and he wrote an essay about it.
But after he returned home, he became ill. One of his last
letters, written to Jiryu at Osaka on the third day, tenth
month, 1783, tells of this.

It is very cold now. I am all the more glad that you
are well. This stupid old man these days has the
unusual pains in the chest and has been troubled.

Most of my heaven-sent life has passed, so soon I expect to cross over to the other side, and I feel forlorn. The other day I went for a mountain walk at Uji, and I will show you some little writings. Why don't you please visit Kyoto; I would like to see you. My wife sends you her greetings, too. I will say more in my next letter.

On the twenty-fourth night of the last month of the year 1783, he asked his disciple Gekkei to write down his last three poems. In the early morning he died, at the age of sixty-seven. We have a record of his last days and death as written by his disciple Kito, who was with him at the time.

The daughter he left behind married again, to a man named Koda, and his widow became a Buddhist nun. She lived for a number of years and, after her death was buried beside Buson in the little cemetery above the temple of Konpukuji, Kyoto, a few yards from the mountainside building known as Basho's Grass Hut, which Buson had helped to rebuild. He had written of this hut and sometimes came there to compose poems with his friends and be in a place where he believed Basho also had been.

For a long time after his death, Buson was principally known as a painter. However, in 1897, an essay was written by the haiku poet Masaoka Shiki in which he compared Basho and Buson and pointed out the merits of the latter as a realist poet. He considered Basho to be more subjective and Buson more objective in their haiku. To him, Buson's writing seemed pictorial. There followed a revived interest in, and appreciation of, Buson the poet.

Throughout Japan today the name of Buson is well known. To his grave come a number of visitors daily, most murmuring aloud to their companions several of his haiku. Special exhibits of his art work, even when in small, out-of-the-way museums, are invariably well attended. Along with his name is usually mentioned that of his revered master Basho, who is frequently considered his almost saintly superior. But Buson himself is remembered and respected as a great man, and to poets, he is still a very important influence.

ESSAYS ON BUSON BY KITO

CONCERNING BUSON'S YOUNGER DAYS

Sometime in the past, in the ninth year of An-ei probably, I visited my master one day at this house "Yahantei." It was a spring twilight with the last remnants of falling cherry blossoms and songs of birds. Rain started to fall quietly, and there happened to be one other guest who intruded into the room. So the master lit a candle with his own hands and sat formally, and said, "Long ago when I was in Edo and all by myself, I tried to search for the inner secret of old master Basho and wrote elegantly, being attracted to the loftiness of *Seedless Chestnuts [Minashiguri]* and *A Winter Day [Fuyu no Hi]* [books done together by Basho and his friends]. But people of the common world didn't know this exquisite world. At that time, I was twenty-seven years old, still young, and yet my poetry was already mature. People of the common world looked at me as though I were their enemy. Once a person gave me advice, saying, 'Haikai is humor. To be in harmony with people and enjoy chatting is best. Your queer eccentric way does not suit *haikai*'s purpose. Why don't you compromise and go the same way as other people?'

"When I heard this, I formed a sort of viewpoint that influenced me when I was in the Kanto provinces. When I was in a place where Bakurin and Shiko were admired, I wrote haiku in these two poets' ways. When I was in an area where Kikaku and Ransetsu were liked, I recited in their styles. When I came to Kyoto, I imitated the ways of Tantan and Rajin. Thus, wherever I went, I was treated properly and my *haikai* were considered matchless. But, to tell the truth, I really ridiculed the common world and scorned the common *haikai*. But it is more than fifty years since I started playing at *haikai*, and now my age is almost seventy, and yet, I am still unable to write *haikai* in a way that satisfies me."

These remarks by Kito, in 1787, were attached to a linked verse poem, or renga, "Momo Sumono" [Peach plum], which had been done by Buson and Kito in 1780.

A Record of Buson's Last Days

Born near the sunlit Naniwa River, he grew up there, spent it many springs and autumns in the bird-crying eastern country, wandered around from place to place in the Oku [northern country], and decided on sunny Kyoto as his permanent dwelling place. In order not to miss seeing anything, he went to the Yosa seacoast. He watched the moon and the snow for three years, around Amano-Hashidate, and then he returned to flowery Kyoto and changed his family name from Taniguchi to Yosa.

Since his childhood, this old man had greatly loved painting, and year after year, he worked to become a master in both the Southern and Northern Sung styles until he finally attained the highest quality in the art of brush and ink. Furthermore, since his youth he had indulged in *haikai* and adored Basho and Kikaku. He also waded in several side streams of *haikai* and matured, with greatness, into a complete freedom of expression in all ways.

In the early part of the Meiwa era (1770), in Kyoto, he took over his master Hajin's work and artistic name and called himself Yahantei.

> "Flower guardian
> although, without bow and arrows,
> a scarecrow!"

On this occasion, many people who admired his *fucho* [wind and tone] entered his gate so hurriedly that they left their shoes untidied at his door. Nevertheless, since he was habitually reluctant to stay in touch with conventionalities, thinking, "On the whole, it is a bother to keep up relationships with people in this world," he closed his gate and hid himself in the painting room and communicated only with those having the same attitude, wanting to remain free to enjoy himself at will.

> "Even more
> because of being alone
> the moon is a friend."

Although his old spirit was relaxed, he muttered General Fukuha's words: "When old, more and more vigorous." Concerning going-staying-sitting-lying and playing-dressing-eating, people said enviously of Buson, "How hale and hearty the old man is! "

He always loved Kyoto's beautiful landscapes and never forgot to view cherry blossoms and the red maple leaves of the eastern suburbs and western mountain. This year, at the end of autumn, being invited by his disciple Mojo, he dragged his walking stick to a place called Tahara, in the farther part of Uji. He let his eyes be pleased with high cliffs, cascading water, odd stones, and strange rocks.

> "A tearing of silk
> streaming out from a biwa
> the voice of autumn."

This was written while recalling Po Chu-i's "Four strings,

one voice, like the tearing of silk cloth."

Thus that autumn passed and the withered winter sky with quiet rainfall; the late crickets sang at the door of his grass hut; wind and morning and evening penetrated through his robes; and about that time his vigor became unsure, stomach pains hurt his old body, and every day he was uncomfortable. Worried people came hurriedly to visit and always remembered to serve him medicine, nursing and taking care of him beyond the ordinary way.

But this sickness of his old age became more serious every day; in spite of the many different remedies given with sincere hearts, there was no effect. So everybody assembled in his hut and, one after another, visited at his sick bed and tried to find ways to comfort his old mind.

One time he called me to come beside his pillow and said, "Recently, I could not forget the matter about the preface to *Gosha-bogu* [Five Ox-cartsful of Writings]. Although my hand trembled and my mind was in confusion, I managed to take up the writing brush. Tell Korekoma [son of the poet for whom the preface was written] at once and let him observe his father's wishes." This was the last brush holding of Buson's life. How deep it was, the karma between Korekoma and his father, and we feel grateful that Buson's preface is not missing from the book.

Also, he once said to his night nurse, "Even being sick like this, my fondness for the way is beyond reason and I try to make haiku. The high stage of 'My dream hovers over withered fields' [Basho's last haiku] is impossible for me to reach.

Therefore, the old poet Basho's greatness is supremely moving to me now."

Thus he taught us as intimately as ever. "This will be worth treasuring," people said when he spoke, feeling pleased at one moment but sore at heart the next.

Then in the middle of December, his inner sickness seemed to be passing out of his body and his suffering appeared to be gradually healing, but he had no appetite, his body and mind were exhausted, and, each day, hope seemed less. Everybody got together and only wished for his good.

With a sincere will, his wife and daughter and others, like Gekkei and Baitei, both in the morning and evening, helped his rising and lying down, but he moaned, especially on the twenty-second and twenty-third nights. People felt extremely downhearted and unsure watching the sick face that we tactfully asked about afterwards. He said, "Well, I have no thoughts about the way I have come. When I was in the remote northern country I became sick while traveling. Once I nearly starved, suffered from coldness and heat. And on several other difficult journeys I often suffered greatly. Now I have been peaceful since settling in the capital, but happening to be bothered by sickness, I am given much medicine and people's sincere heartfelt care. How deep the karma was! This stupid old man's wishes are all fulfilled. But my daughter has no worldly connections, and the matter of her future lingers in my mind. Perhaps after I go, two or three of you people may show her kindness. Well, concern over things will get in the way of passing on with a peaceful mind," and he pulled the quilt over his face without saying more. Unable to do anything, the people remained sitting nearby.

On the night of the twenty-fourth, his sick body was very calm, and his speaking became natural again. Quietly he called Gekkei near him and said, "I made some poems during my sickness. Write them down quickly. " Brush and inkstone were prepared with haste.

When we were ready for his voice, he recited:

> "Winter *uguisu*—
> long ago in Wang Wei's
> garden hedge too!
>
> *Uguisu!*
> What is that rustling?
> Frost on the bushes."

And still he seemed to be trying to say another piece. After a while,

> "With white plum blossoms
> these nights to the faint light of dawn
> are turning.

"For this one you should put the title 'Early Spring'."

These three haiku were the last of his life; he passed on as though sleeping peacefully; it was a blessed going.

The sorrow of his daughter and her mother was beyond

expression. At that time, we friends, who had gathered together making no distinction between day and night, were sick and agitated with grief, but in vain. Eventually, at dawn, we knocked at the doors of close friends and informed them of his passing. Denpuku, Hyakuchi, Gasoku, Kado, Joshitsu, Soshu, Gyokan, Shuba, and other familiar people came running immediately. Close affection while he was alive, the helplessness of death's separation, no words of farewell, made people cry in bewilderment.

Although wanting to leave everything just as it was, in accordance with his wishes, we got rid of the night quilts and spread out a fresh woolen mat. And we chose one of his daily robes, which was clean, and fixed its neck-binding. On top of it we put the usual robe of the dead Buddha, hooded him with a thin cloth, and dressed him as though he were a live person. We placed him with head to the north, face to the west, lying on his right side. We burned incense, offered flowers, received the temple priest, and each of us chanted a Nembutsu [Namu Amida Butsu]. Then we quietly changed the dead body into smoke. At that time, people everywhere were preparing for the New Year celebration, and as we did not want to disturb busy people nor have the news ignored by those who tried to avoid hearing unfortunate events during the holidays, we pretended Buson was still in his sickbed and did not publicly announce his passing away until around the time when New Year pine tree decorations were taken away. Then, from the neighboring countryside and nearby villages, Buson's disciples came hurrying as fast as their legs could carry them. With no distinction between intimate and non-intimate, acquaintances and old friends, they came to mourn and crowded the grass hut. On the twenty-fifth day of the first moon, with the utmost propriety, a funeral was held for the second time.

Buson's ashes were buried just outside the hedge of Basho's grass hut by the temple of Konpukuji and to show his lasting veneration to the soul of old Basho, a simple egg-shaped stone was placed over them.

> When I die
> I shall be next to his stone—
> withered pampas grass.

Buson often expressed his appreciation of the serene landscape of this mountainside. A new *uguisu* bird playing in a willow tree, a *hototogisu* bird passing over a gate and roofs, deer on a mountain trail, snow on a farmhouse— these things go along naturally with Buson's paintings.

The moon that rises above the eastern mountains shines forever as the way of Buddha's teaching. Trees and bushes in the garden give fragrance eternally, endlessly offering flowers to the Buddha. These, also, are non-temporary karma.

This description of Buson's last days and nights serves the purpose of helping his followers recollect and adore the old master. While thinking thus, I write with my foolish brush on the day of the fifth week after the funeral, in this revered temple where we just held a ceremony to comfort the old master's soul.

> Sincerely written by Kito
> at Rakuto [eastern Kyoto],
> Temple of Konpuku,
> under the mortuary
> tablet of Buson.

This personal account of the last months of Buson's life (Yahan o Shuen ki) was written after Buson's death in 1784, by his disciple Kito. It is included in the book Karahiba, a haiku collection made in mourning for Buson soon after his death. The book also contains Chinese poems, renga, and essays composed by a number of his disciples and friends.

9 781893 996816